TRIBES

TRIBES

DESMOND MORRIS
PETER MARSH

PYRAMID BOOKS

Foreword © Desmond Morris 1988

Text © Peter Marsh 1988

First published in 1988 by Pyramid
an imprint of the Octopus Publishing Group
Michelin House, 81 Fulham Road, London SW3 6RB

ISBN: 1–871307–18–X

Produced by the Justin Knowles Publishing Group
9 Colleton Crescent, Exeter, Devon EX2 4BY, UK

Designer: Ron Pickless

Picture Researcher: Suzanne Williams

Phototypeset by Keyspools Limited, Golborne, Lancs
Printed and bound in Italy

CONTENTS

FOREWORD

Man is a tribal animal. We must fully appreciate this fact if we are to understand one of the most important facets of human nature. To ignore it or deny it – as so many priests and politicians do – is to court disaster. The tribal qualities of the human species colour almost every aspect of our social lives. They are so basic to us that, were we ever to lose them, it would mean that we had mutated into another species altogether.

Our tribalism began millions of years ago with our monkey ancestors. All the evidence suggests they did not live in pairs, like nesting birds, but instead moved about in semi-nomadic groups. At dusk they all slept near one another; at dawn they set off together in search of food. In the heat of the day the adults rested and groomed one another while the youngsters played. There was little division of labour, each adult finding food for himself or herself without any aid from the others. Only when the group was threatened by a predator would this condition change: the strongest males of the group might gang up against the attacker and try to drive it off with combined threats. In this behaviour we see the seeds of the later developments tribalism.

It is generally believed that such monkey groups were strictly herbivorous. However, while it is true that they did survive largely on fruits, nuts, berries and roots, they also ate any small animal they could find or subdue. Large insects, young mammals, small birds, lizards and eggs were always favoured supplements to the herbivorous diet, providing valuable proteins, minerals and vitamins. Occasionally some of the larger males would manage to catch and kill a more impressive mammal, such as a young fawn. We know from studies of today's baboons and chimpanzees in the wild that, when this happens, an entirely new feeding pattern appears: food-sharing. For monkeys, both ancient and modern, this has always been a minor aspect of their daily social lives. It is a rarity, but the fact that it occurs at all is highly significant, for it marks the origins of that most crucial human characteristic – active cooperation.

As this meat-eating element of the social lives of our primeval ancestors grew more important, it had a profound effect on our social organization. In order to feast on bigger and bigger prey, groups of the strongest males had to set off on organized expeditions. Only by helping one another in an intelligent and planned manner were they able to defeat the larger animals and so provide a feast of high-protein flesh. This momentous step, which allowed man the hunter to evolve out of his monkey ancestry, was taken at least a million years ago. It led to a whole host of dramatic changes in both our physical attributes and our mental condition.

The first of these concerned our size. We grew bigger and stronger as we tackled more and more powerful prey. We also became bipedal. Many people seem to think of bipedalism as a way of speeding up our chases in pursuit of prey, but this is incorrect: the transition to bipedal locomotion actually slowed us down slightly. Nevertheless, it did confer to huge advantages. We were able to see above the long grasses of the plains where we hunted and, even more importantly, we were able to carry weapons. Moreover, at the end of a successful hunt, we were able to carry home the spoils. The practice of transporting the prey to a safe place where it could be shared out with the females and young was another major step towards the modern human condition.

Carrying food home meant that there had to *be* a home, and this was a very novel idea for our ancestors. They had to give up their nomadic ways and settle down at a fixed abode. There the pregnant and nursing females, the elderly members of the group and the youngsters could remain in comparative safety while the gang of adult males set off on a long chase, searching for, trapping and killing a large prey animal. This major division of labour – the females rearing the young and in their spare time searching for fruits and roots like their monkey ancestors, and the males scouring the countryside in hunting bands – is thought to have been at least partly responsible for the development of a slightly different temperament and personality between the early human males and females. The males had a much stronger urge to belong to an active, risk-taking "pack" while, although the females were highly sociable back at the village base, they did not evolve such a powerful sense of gang-membership.

This ganging up by the adult males of the group was like the formation of a minor tribe within a major one.

The whole group – men, women and children – were all members of the main tribe, or social unit. They knew their place in the community and recognized everyone else by name and by face. But within this arrangement there was the male sub-tribe with its own special rules and its more tightly organized structure. For them it was crucial that there should be mutual trust and group loyalty. One mistake or carelessness by any member of the male pack could ruin an entire hunt strategy, risk the lives of his colleagues and leave the whole tribe suffering the pains of hunger. The pressure was on, and the males' behaviour had to evolve quickly to ensure that this brave new world of chasing and killing was efficiently planned and that their predatory raids were properly executed. Survival of the whole tribe would often depend upon it, and so natural selection swiftly eliminated any early human group that failed as hunters.

This state of affairs lasted for about 50,000 generations, and then came a further dramatic stage in our social development: we usually refer to it as the Agricultural revolution, and it occurred only 500 generations ago. It all started with a new feeding pattern – not food-sharing this time, but food-storing. As soon as we became efficient enough to enjoy a food surplus we had to find ways of storing it for use during the long winter months, or for lean times when the pickings were scarce. With food-storing came farming and the improvement of crops. We began to modify natural foods and make them more accessible to us. The wild animals that came to prey upon these new, improved foodstuffs were caught and penned. Domestication of animals became common practice, with the result that hunting was no longer necessary. The more efficient method of keeping and breeding the animals in captivity, then slaughtering them when they were needed for food, became rapidly established about 10,000 years ago. The ease with which this made food available gave rise to a new human commodity: leisure. It is striking that, right from the start, back at the beginning of the Neolithic period, this new-found leisure was used in a very special way. Almost immediately it was given over to hunting activities. Although the practical need to hunt for food was gone, there remained a psychological need. In short, the adult males found it hard to give up hunting, and so they invented sport-hunting.

The sport-hunts of the ancients took up an amazing amount of their time and energy. While the growth of farming helped to streamline our societies, the spare time was almost exclusively taken up with activities that were little more than symbolic re-enactments of our primeval hunting past. The prey was now frequently inedible, but that did not matter. The chase was the thing. Men needed the excitement of it. The urge to hunt had been built into the very core of their beings.

Much later on, when cities started to spring up, urban males found themselves in a quandary. Crowded together in huge numbers, they had nowhere to hunt. Their country cousins were still able to chase across fields and through woods, often on horseback, and the hunts could continue (as they still do, of course, in many rural parts of the modern world). But the urbanites needed something in their place. The answer came in the form of the arena. All across the ancient city world, huge stadia were constructed where animals could be attacked and killed – a new kind of "display hunt" without the chase. From the Colosseum of ancient Rome to the bullrings of modern Spain, this corrupted form of hunting created new heroes and attracted vast crowds of human tribesmen, desperate to become involved in a group hunting activity, even if it was only a debased version of the proud food-seeking original.

With the passage of years, this bloodthirsty form of ritual hunting has gradually been replaced by two new kinds of hunt: one physical and one mental. The physical version is what we today call sport. All forms of sport are either ritualized aiming or ritualized chasing, or a combination. They take these elements of the hunt and then direct them towards a symbolic prey – targets replacing the animal victims, bull's-eyes replacing the bulls. And the tribesmen are still there to soak up the thrills. Like their primitive counterparts they show passionate loyalty, distinctive adornments and all the trappings of the hunting pack. They discuss their exploits endlessly, and in great detail, as they have always done. The sportsmen and their followers are the closest analogue we have today to the age-old human tribal hunters.

Less close, but even more important, are the "mental hunters", those individuals who have abandoned the physical aspects of the hunt and transformed it into a purely symbolic activity. The business tribe hunts a contract; the academic tribe hunts a new theory; the engineering tribe hunts a new invention; the literary tribe hunts a new masterpiece. Each in its own way follows the ancient imperatives: only the nature of targets has been changed. The new tribesmen talk about their aims, but their aims have become their ambitions. Abstract targets have replaced real ones, just as real targets replaced animal prey in the gradual development of the human tribesmen.

Tribalism is, however, a double-edged sword. The tribal feelings are in themselves quite neutral, but they can be used for good or ill, constructively or destructively. Given half a chance, they will be employed to good effect, but if the tribal urges of a particular group are frustrated they are likely to find an alternative and often damaging outlet. They cannot be suppressed because they are too basic and so, if the ruling authorities in any society deny the expression of tribalism in a helpful way, the young males will not simply remain calm and passive. Instead, they will form unofficial tribes and attack the culture which has attempted to cut them off from their primeval inheritance.

This process can be seen at work wherever gangs of alienated young males gather. They form gangs of muggers, thugs and hooligans, and then proceed to express all their pent-up tribal feelings against the police, the military or any other manifestation of conformist authority. The excitement is the same – the planning and the tactics, the strategies and the schemes, the risks and the skin-tingling dangers, the escapades and the endless story-telling about those escapades. The whole tribal scene is recreated out of nothing – or, rather, out of the chaos of their oppressed lives.

So in the end the tribal games are just the same, regardless of whether the groups concerned are establishment-backed or rebels: fox-hunters or football hooligans, commandos or criminals, trades unionists of terrorists, Boy Scouts or Hell's Angels. All obey basically the same rules. We hate those who oppose us and praise those who support us, yet often we do not realize how close the different tribes are in their structure, their role-playing and their displays.

Modern tribal tendencies are everywhere around us: in our committees, our juries, our teams and our squads; in our councils, our governments, our board-members, our clubs; in our secret societies, our protest groups, our clans, our institutes; and in our childhood gangs and our pop-group fan clubs. Without the adventurous, risk-taking, active cooperation and organizational restraint that operates within each of these groups we would not have been able to build our civilizations and we would never have gone to the moon. On the dark side, we would also have avoided war – a sad, violent corruption of our tribal urges and group loyalties – and all the other forms of aggressive disruption, from the most savage forms of terrorism to the mildest of group protests. But, despite these unfortunate aspects of the tribal urge, it remains one of our great assets, and so, if we are to enjoy the creative fruits of the motivating force of the tribal imperative, we must be prepared to run a constant risk of disaster. We can never live without it as long as we remain human, so it is better that we learn to live with it and exploit its amazing potential, a potential that has in a mere ten millennia carried us from the Stone Age to the Space Age.

Desmond Morris

INTRODUCTION

The origins of the tribe lie in the earliest stages of human evolution. The patterns of organized agriculture which first produced modern nations and states are only 10,000 years old – a mere tick of the evolutionary clock. By contrast, the emergence of Man as a hunter-gatherer, the unique pattern of social behaviour which led immediately to a tribal way of life, occurred some five million years ago.

The principal difference between the earliest hominids and their primate ancestors was that they ate flesh. As time passed, meat was increasingly obtained through hunting rather than through scavenging. As the early hunter's ambitions increased and his typical prey became larger, there evolved a pattern of cooperative behaviour within small groups: a band of 6–8 males could trap and kill much more effectively together than could the same number of hunters acting as individuals.

The hunting band was an effective, adaptive solution to the survival and development of a partly carnivorous species. A group of 6–8 hunting males implied a typical band size of about 25, including women and children. However, while this unit could provide for efficient hunting, it was too small for social and reproductive stability. For example, simply to ensure a balance between the rates of birth of boys and girls – essential when a band relied on the activities of male hunters – a larger unit of social organization was required. The ideal population of such a unit seems to have settled at about 500 men, women and children. And so emerged the tribe, typically embracing 20 hunting bands, each consisting of about six families.

From the tribes that survive today in various parts of the world (often unnecessarily referred to as "primitive" peoples) we can gain some idea of the complex social structures and patterns of traditional behaviour engendered by the tribal way of life. For example, the !Kung Bushmen of the Kalahari continue the traditions of past millennia in their semi-nomadic lifestyle, which still revolves around the hunting of wild animals and the gathering of local plants. When the plant stock is used up or game becomes scarce in one locality, bands move to other territories. The origins of basic human behaviour patterns – territoriality, marriage and kinship, adaptive taboos, styles of social interaction, and so on – are demonstrated in such tribes just as our evolutionary past is revealed in the fossils of fish, reptiles and birds.

Traditional tribes are, however, fast disappearing from our planet. "Civilization" has with ruthless efficiency waged a genocidal war against tribal cultures. Those that remain are often herded into reservations which have so few natural resources that the tribal population diminishes to a point where eventual extinction is inevitable. Alternatively, tribes are seduced away from their traditional lifestyles by the false promises of 20th-century technological societies.

Nevertheless, as the "primitive" mode of living vanishes, tribalism lives on. The larger and more heterogeneous modern societies become, the more people are inclined to recreate the tribe: they fashion for themselves natural units in which a sense of "belonging" is still possible.

Man's early hunting ancestry was not responsible, as some have gloomily suggested, for his emergence as a lustful killer of members of his own species: "civilization" has done that. Rather, hunting generated a need for cooperative bonds and personal ties, enshrined in the traditions and mores of tribal culture. It is to these fundamental social patterns that people all over the world return in response to the contradictions and novel stresses of dehumanized societies. In modern tribes – the tribal groupings of the 20th century – we rediscover our true heritage as human beings.

Peter Marsh

1 TRIBAL BONDING

The word "tribe" conjures up in most people's minds images of "primitive" societies, near-naked warriors and mystical ceremonies. Or perhaps we think of the North American Indians, whose history has been so dramatically misportrayed by Hollywood movies. Tribalism, to most of us, represents an earlier stage in the evolution of the human race – something which came to an end with the advent of "civilization". Those societies still organized along tribal lines are viewed as interesting subject material for anthropological study, but it occurs to few people that they can provide significant models for patterns of human behaviour in the 20th century – and, for that matter, the 21st.

Yet tribalism has never disappeared, however much the societies in which we live may be removed from those of our hunter-gatherer ancestors. Because we are essentially social animals, we have a drive to establish particular forms of affiliation with other people. We might be American, British, French or Australian, but identification solely with others of our own nationality is not in itself enough: it is too abstract, and it lacks the sense of true bonding which can be established only in the context of smaller groups. So, as our national units become increasingly large and heterogeneous, we recreate social units on a more human scale. Even in the anonymous societies of our major conurbations, people band together to create modern tribes which share the basic features of traditional ones.

Anthropologists define a tribe as a collection of groups of people who share patterns of speech, basic cultural characteristics and, in the traditional sense, a common territory. The most important feature, however, is that members of a tribe feel that they have more in common with each other than with neighbouring groups. This sense of communality both binds the members of a tribe together and distances them from non-members of the tribe.

Many traditional tribes lack centralized authority. The adult members (often only the males) share in decision-making and all have roughly equal status. Such tribes are known as "acephalous" societies, meaning that they have no single head. Political organization is often based on kinship networks and alliances between extended family or clan groupings. Even where there are marked differences in status, such as between males and females or between adults and juveniles, there tends to be a clear sense of equality within age or gender groups. The Yako of Nigeria provide a textbook example of an acephalous tribal society. Each village has a distinct autonomy and is further divided into the equivalent of local wards. Every mature male adult is expected to play a role in the administration of the community, and power and authority are devolved through kinship lineages and groupings based on age.

Chiefdoms, by contrast, have more clearly centralized authority. This serves to integrate the various communities that make up the tribal society. Social stratification is usually more pronounced than in acephalous societies, and the roles of kinship and intermarriage are more important in the political process. Even in such cultures, however, there is much less role-specialization than in

modern societies. While rank and privilege are evident, there is a much greater sense of "belonging" among all tribal members, whatever their status position, and a distinctive feeling of common purpose.

The tribal structure, acephalous or not, provides a framework in which individuals have a clear concept of social identity. Social identity is to do with knowing who we are in relation to other people. There is a basic human need to feel that we share with an identifiable group of people around us particular habits, values, attitudes and styles of behaviour; complementarily, we need to feel distinct from other groups whose characteristics are quite different. In traditional societies, this kind of social identity is unavoidable. Tribal customs, folklore, rituals and ceremonies marking the transition from one role to another – all of these ensure that each member feels inextricably bound to the culture in which he or she has been born. Within these social frameworks a high degree of conformity is expected, but there is also the opportunity for a sense of genuine independence. Putting it another way, in all cultures becoming an individual, in the true sense of that word, necessitates first becoming "one of the boys" (or girls).

Rock concerts are often opportunities for individuals to feel part of a well-defined collective, sharing similar levels of emotional arousal and patterns of behaviour. Quite distinctive tribal activity is displayed at this Sham 69 concert (*above*). The new young dealers in the City (*top*), the financial "hunters" of modern societies, are equally tribal in their patterns of affiliation and behaviour.

AGE SETS

While tribalism's most vivid manifestations in modern societies take the form of distinct social groupings and subcultures, each with their characteristic identities and patterns of social bonding, our mainstream cultures as a whole

Above
Becoming a member of a tribe in a modern society can involve a gradual transition, reflected in overall style and behaviour. The young boy in this picture of a grouse-shooting party in Yorkshire is beginning not only to dress like his elders but also to adopt their posture.

Left
A typical arena for male tribal bonding in Mediterranean countries is the café bar. Here a group of Turks meet to enjoy water-pipes and engage in ''men's talk''.

Opposite
Despite the views of some male anthropologists, collective bonding is not solely the preserve of men. Here Samburu girls in Kenya reinforce the stable links between them as they sing tribal songs around the fire in their hut.

Above
Japanese business-management training is organized along distinctly tribal lines, as seen here at the Fuji School. Trainees pass through an initiation ceremony where they kneel in rows and 17 ribbons of shame are attached to their smocks – each one denoting some discipline to be fulfilled in order to graduate. The humbling process demands that trainees perform servile and useless tasks, such as picking grass from the lawns with their fingers. This whole ritualized process is aimed at discouraging individuality and reinforcing loyalty and obedience to the company.

Right
Boys at the Totem Pole School in Japan. The principal, Isao Kawashima, operates what he calls a "primal" system. Boys (there are no girls at the school) leave behind their normal life and their individuality when they change into loincloths in the locker room. Along with standard academic subjects, the boys are exposed to vigorous exercise and hardship in their collective pursuit of high standards.

share certain important features with traditional societies. One social element which provides for a degree of identity is known as "age grouping" or "age grades".

Japanese workers at the Matsushita Electric Company singing their firm's song.

In every society, whether traditional or modern, age is used as an indicator of the roles which a person is expected to play. In Western cultures, for example, we restrict certain activities, such as the consumption of liquor, to those over a certain age. Becoming legally an adult is a matter solely of attaining a given chronological status. Subsequently, we pass through various age-related status positions – middle-aged, elderly, retired, etc. At each point we tend to form bonds and affiliations more readily with other members of the particular age set we have reached than with members of other age sets. Teenagers bond with other teenagers; the elderly find new opportunities for social ties in the clubs and institutions which cater for them.

Even within the various age sets, further identity-related distinctions are created. School classes, selection for which is based principally on the ages of the pupils, give rise not only to enduring social groupings but also to elaborate patterns of seniority and juniority. At university, students become part of the "class of '88", or whatever the year in which they expect to graduate. This tag stays with them long afterwards, prompting reunions many years later of people who feel that special ties unite them.

In traditional cultures the role of age sets is even more clearly defined. Among the Nuer of East Africa, for example, the relative position of any male is

Above
The Japanese Yakuza signal their tribal allegiance through highly elaborate tattoos.

Opposite
Male bonding brings with it hostility towards, and rivalry with, other groups. Here, this inevitable consequence of "in-group" affiliations is safely channelled through a tug-of-war contest.

determined solely by the age group to which he belongs. For his entire life every Nuer man remains a member of the group of other males with whom he was initiated into the tribe. He is always junior to those who became adult members of the society before him, and he will maintain seniority over those who followed him. He will never be able to have sexual relations with the daughter of an age-mate, since she is his "daughter" as well. His commitments to his equals are clearly defined, as are his obligations to his elders, which he will always be expected to meet.

The effect of the age-set system is quite profound. It creates a distinct set of loyalties which are totally independent of family ties. It provides a way of distributing both authority and labour, and gives both young and old clearly defined roles which are suited to the capabilities of their age level. It causes young men to act together in important ways, such as in the defence of their country, while leaving most of the decision-making to their elders, whose physical capabilities no longer allow them to take such an active part in the society. Most importantly, it provides for the development of distinct "communities" of people at all stages in their lives.

VOLUNTARY GROUPINGS

Age sets are, of course, essentially non-voluntary groupings. We do not choose our date of birth, and therefore our bondings to others of the same age are purely a matter of chance. Many traditional societies offer no alternative to such

Formal dress uniforms of guests at an Austrian Opera Ball.

arrangements: the tribal units are often of a size such that each individual can feel that he or she is a full and active member of the culture as a whole and needs little else as a key in order to carve out a social identity. There are, however, certain exceptions. For example, discrete warrior groupings existed within the North American Indian cultures. The Cheyenne had five such organizations, each with its own leader, dress and rituals, and loyalties to the organization cut across both kinship and age-set ties. In some of the smaller South American and Liberian cultures we find secret societies and religious cults which have characteristics similar to those of the North American Indian groupings.

It is in the larger societies, however, where the national unit does not promote strong feelings of direct involvement, that voluntary associations are most frequently established in order to recreate units of a more human scale. The growth of urbanization and industrialization since the turn of the century has led to the rapid development of highly impersonal environments in which a sense of neighbourhood is difficult to achieve. As a response, the natural human drive for affiliation has spawned a vast range of voluntary organizations. To a large extent these have replaced the multipurpose groupings based on kinship and clan allegiances which still flourish in rural and less industrialized settings.

The role of such associations is clearly seen in the newly developed regions of Third World countries. In the Peruvian capital Lima, for example, poor migrants from the harsh rural areas established tightly knit organizations based on regional origins. These served to provide newcomers with support and the sense of belonging which would otherwise have been lost as they made the transition from subsistence farming to industrial labour. Such organizations have also played a vital role as pressure groups, demanding fair treatment from employers and adequate resources from the government.

In West Africa we likewise find many examples of recreated tribes in the newly developed cities. They are instrumental in preserving tribal traditions, rituals and habits in settings which may appear to be a little incongruous. Industrialization and economic development, far from destroying tribal ways of life, have both fostered the re-establishment of traditional groups and generated quite new ones.

The tribal unions of West Africa have parallels in North America. Ethnic pride among the Indian populations has developed considerably over the past decade, and many associations have developed to further the cultural interests and identity of these peoples. The Crow Indian Tobacco Society, for example, encourages a sense of mystical belonging among the descendants of this once famous and proud culture. The Kwakiutl Indians of British Columbia continue to practise their secret rituals despite their integration into mainstream Canadian society. The Pueblo Indians have their Katchina cults, which ensure the continuance of the essential rituals of tribal life.

However, many of the voluntary associations in modern cultures are concerned less with the maintenance of old tribal customs and affiliations than with the creation of new ones. Their ostensible functions may be as diverse as pigeon racing or the organization of mock military battles, but all provide for social bonding and are most frequently established as antidotes to the impersonal nature of modern urban settings.

MALE AND FEMALE ORGANIZATIONS

The most common associations in which collective activities are restricted to

those who are recognized members have traditionally been either all-male in composition or at least male-dominated. This, it has been proposed, reflects the fact that, during the hunter-gatherer stage of our cultural evolution, the period when the tribe emerged as a social unit, it was the males who needed to establish the closest bonds – simply in order to hunt more effectively. While the males took part in the hunt, a cooperative venture, women were largely assigned roles which were far more individualistic. Child-rearing and gathering locally available vegetables and fruits were tasks which could be accomplished successfully without the need for collective, collaborative action. Therefore, it is suggested, the men bonded but the women did not.

This hypothesis has some merit, and can partly account for the fact that most of our cultures are still male-dominated. It can also go some way towards explaining why so few traditional cultures are truly matriarchal. Yet the issue of whether the male bonding tendency is firmly rooted in our genetic makeup, or whether it has been passed down to us through the cultural transmission of societal norms, is more difficult to resolve – and perhaps it does not need to be resolved. What is clear is that, although women have traditionally been excluded from closed associations and have had little opportunity to establish their own tribal bonds, they are today making up for this through the creation of groupings as diverse as feminist-oriented political organizations and, in Britain, Women's Institutes.

Typical patterns of female bonding are to be found in youth gangs in the United States. Although these girls will tend to have rather stereotyped roles within their gang, often performing "womanly" duties for the benefit of the men, they also experience a strong attachment to each other and to their collective.

One of the most distinctive female tribes in Britain over the last few years has been the Greenham Women, a stable group permanently encamped outside the United States Air Force base at Greenham Common in Berkshire. Their function has been to maintain the protest against the deployment of nuclear cruise missiles and to campaign for the removal of all nuclear weapons from Britain. The validity or otherwise of their moral and political stance is not for debate here. What are of interest, however, are the "sisterhood" and the close mutual bonds formed between and among the women involved. The Greenham Women provide a clear example of how tribal affiliation is by no means a male prerogative.

The women of Greenham Common are dismissed by many people as an esoteric anomaly – a group of lesbians seeking a way to express their hatred of men. While it is the case that some of the women in the Greenham tribe are indeed lesbians, and some show a distinct antipathy towards males of every description, their determination and their ability to live semi-permanently in the cold and damp conditions of the common have won grudging respect even from those who oppose their political views.

Women's Institutes, by contrast, are far more heterogeneous in their composition and have a quite different place in mainstream society, yet they display the basic principles of female bonding every bit as clearly as do the Greenham Women. Women's Institutes are widely regarded, even by many women themselves, as concerned solely with traditionally female activities – bottling fruit, making jam, weaving rugs and engaging in other "homely" domestic practices. The reality of the WI, however, is rather different. With 352,000 members (1988), it is the most powerful female collective in Britain: run on efficient, democratic lines, it should be the envy of many male associations.

At the local level, the WI provides opportunities for like-minded women to belong to a highly distinctive social group with a sense of sorority lacking in most other areas of modern societies. Members bear witness to the sense of belonging which is achieved not only in the branches but across the entire network of local associations. The WI's journal, *Home and Country*, regularly features letters from previously lonely and isolated women who report that their lives have been changed by the new-found opportunities for collective involvement.

This increasing role of women in the development of modern tribes suggests that our evolutionary past and the history of our development as cultural animals do not necessarily dictate or restrict the patterns of our social activities and relationships. Genetic factors and deep aspects of heritage most certainly influence the ways in which we organize our societies, whether they be traditional or modern, but they do not limit the social potential of either men or women. The universal human need for people to realize themselves as individuals through collective unity with like-minded persons is not restricted to one half of our species.

SOCIAL GROUPINGS IN MODERN SOCIETIES

Many modern societies are now fast approaching their limits in terms of size and the impersonality which that size creates. Increasingly we witness violent reactions in massive urban developments to the alienation experienced by their inhabitants. Many young people, in particular, find no source of identity or sense of belonging in a world which often disowns them, and so turn increasingly to

Opposite
Distinctive forms of symbolic dress are by no means confined to lower-class youth culture groups. These Daughters of the Revolution in the United States express their allegiances and lifestyles with equal eloquence in their style of clothing.

Sloane Rangers are an instantly recognizable English upper-class tribe. The waxed jackets and green wellington boots are their hallmark.

alternative youth cultures in which they can be *somebody*. In the harshness of economic recession, this quest for identity, coupled with the anger engendered by disadvantage, is expressed in the aggression of the youth gang or in declarations of solidarity which require a clearly defined enemy. Racism, anti-Semitism, and other types of victimization of "out-groups" occur when a sense of frustration is fuelled by feelings of anonymity and detachment. For some members of our 20th-century cultures, the only way of fully understanding themselves is to establish whom they are against.

While on the one hand a sense of injustice and disenchantment gives rise to tribalism, sometimes with destructive consequences, the same drive for social bonding is equally evident among the more affluent and successful members of our societies – so much so that social labelling among the new professional groups has become increasingly common. The term "Yuppie" (young, upwardly mobile professional) originated in the 1980s in the United States as a description of a new breed of rising entrepreneurs. Once the term had been coined, people started to identify with this distinctive label and positively to aspire to the lifestyle it denoted. Soon the Yuppies became a tribe of people with similar jobs, style of language, interests, tastes and attitudes. The Filofax, or "personal organizer", became more than just a high-priced diary and address book: now it was a symbol of allegiance to a cultural unit.

In the wake of the Yuppies have come other middle-class tribes, each with

H. EDWARD PIETZE III

equally distinctive acronymic nicknames, and it is now fashionable to describe people in terms of their social tribe. Up-market glossy magazines regularly carry features informing their readers about the current labels and the groups to which they refer. Although such articles are usually quite trivial, they reveal the rising need for people to define themselves in terms of their lifestyles and to feel a sense of affiliation with those who share them.

In Britain, this trend towards tribal definitions and labels was undoubtedly given a boost by Peter York and his reported "discovery" of the Sloane Rangers – affluent young people who lived in fashionable areas such as that around London's Sloane Square. Writing with an appropriate sense of cynicism, he described the world of this particular section of British upper-middle-class society in the way an anthropologist might talk of a distinctive African culture. Sloanes could be identified by the fact that they wore green wellington boots and waxed jackets, drove Golf GTIs and virtually lived out their lives in wine bars. A simplistic but not totally inaccurate caricature, this description soon became much more of a reality as young people in that stratum of society identified themselves with the image and adopted both the Sloane style and the attitudes that went with it.

Young Fogeys have of course always been around in the rarefied atmosphere of Oxford, Cambridge, Harvard and other "prestige" universities, but it was only in the 1980s that the name began to be applied. Their reactionary views,

Middle-aged matrons in full costume at the Kentucky Derby.

Above
While males utilize pop concerts for the expression of collective aggression, girls and women give vent to other emotions. The idolization of the performers reaches hysterical proportions in the highly charged atmosphere of large groups.

Left
Revival meetings and concerts are opportunities not only for nostalgia and sentimentality but also for a sense of belonging with other like-minded people. Here the 1950s are celebrated through style of dress, dance and collective values and ideals.

Opposite
Pop festivals in the open air serve as opportunities for overt expressions of collective unity, even in the rain. Here at the San Bernadino rock concert in California, organized by the chairman of Apple Computers, Stephen Wozniak, group aggression surfaces amid the celebrations.

traditional styles of dress and feigned disinterest in the real world of work and the professions typified them, and their distinctiveness was reinforced by the emergence of brash, stylish and energetic groups of upstarts.

Yuppies were, and still are, the antithesis of the establishment order, relying on their talents and business acumen rather than on inherited wealth or the old school tie. It is through such clear contrasts that tribal unity is made concrete. While the Yuppie, the Sloane and the Young Fogey do indeed have common interests and values, this commonality is enhanced by the experience of distance from other clearly defined collectives. As one tribe emerges, others are spawned in its shadow.

Dinkies, for example, emerged as a Yuppie splinter group, embracing an especially single-minded segment of the new professional classes. "Double Income, No Kids" couples were able to carve out a particularly identifiable stylish lifestyle because their considerable disposable income was not squandered on raising offspring and sending them to smart schools. In contrast were the Drabbies, the staid but ideologically sound tribe with several children and socially useful jobs as teachers, social workers, etc. Yummies (Young Urban Mothers), Swells (Single Women Earning Lots in London) and Spoolers (Stripped Pine, Olive Oil, Laura Ashley) also became the subject of dinner-table talk.

While the terms used to describe such tribes are rather ephemeral, they reflect the ever-increasing need for people to define themselves as members of distinct subgroups of the population. The reality of such groupings is revealed not only in the plethora of labels but more directly in new trends in market-research techniques. In order to market and sell goods effectively, major companies have to identify particular segments of the population and target their advertising accordingly. There is little point, for example, in advertising expensive designer-label jewellery in mass-circulation magazines bought by people who cannot possibly afford such luxury items; by contrast, an advertisement placed in a low-circulation "quality" magazine may produce an impressive response. Increasingly, however, the marketing people are finding that the traditional demographic measures, based primarily on social class and income levels, are not sufficiently sensitive or sophisticated. The aim of the newer methods is to identify the social tribes to which people belong and the size and characteristic features of each of those tribes. Known as "values and lifestyles analysis", the approach is little interested in knowledge simply of people's income or social background: that does not permit a sufficient distinction between the various types of potential customer, and nor does it predict with any degree of accuracy which newspapers people read, what they watch on television, or the range of articles they might be interested in purchasing.

Identifying people in terms of the discrete social groupings they belong to, defined in terms of aspirations, tastes, values and particular lifestyles, allows marketing departments to determine very easily the size of the market for various products and the channels through which advertising should be directed. Where there are several segments of the population to whom a particular product might appeal, the manner in which an item is advertised can be tailored to each of them so that it appeals directly to their tribal affiliations.

This commercial realization of patterns of collective bonding is, perhaps, the best evidence for tribalism in modern societies. We may make jokes about the names of trendy middle-class groupings, or prefer to think of ourselves as free, independent spirits, owing allegiance to no group in particular, but most of us in actuality find it hard to escape categorization. Modern tribes consist not merely of the ostentatious youth cults, with their elaborate hairstyles and seemingly perverse tastes in clothing. Nor is it only members of esoteric institutions, secret societies, clubs and associations who strive to achieve distinctive collective unity. All of us rely on others for our sense of self and identity. Where the scale of our culture denies us a true sense of belonging, we conspire to scale things down – to create units in which we can be human. In other words, tribes.

TERRITORIES

Territoriality is such a deeply ingrained aspect of human life that we tend to assume that it is something we have acquired during our evolution. There are many books which deal with our "territorial instincts", comparing our behaviour with those of animals as diverse as Siamese fighting fish, wildebeest and baboons. The human animal's "biological" urge to defend its home territory lies, it is suggested, at the root of Man's aggression and violence.

However, the connection between territoriality and aggression is not quite as simple as that. Although some species of animals always show territorial defence behaviours, many others do so only if the ecology is such that there is a need to defend access to scarce resources. In traditional human cultures we likewise find considerable variations in the extent to which large-scale territories, with distinct boundaries akin to those of national units, are established and the degree to which they are defended. Again, these variations are usually products of identifiable ecological and economic factors. What is common, however, to all human societies is their need for a sense of "place" – a feeling of living in an environment which has boundaries and identity.

Concern with territoriality of this kind predates modern societies by several millennia. To choose a single example, the Romans had a god named Terminus whose responsibility it was to reign over land boundaries. Throughout the Empire, individual and group territories were marked with Termini stones on which a likeness of the god was carved. Homes in both the Greek and Roman cultures of the ancient world were separated by at least three feet: the space in between belonged not to any individual but to the gods.

Moving to more recent history, in England during the 15th and 16th centuries annual ceremonies such as Rogationtide were conducted in order to reaffirm village and property boundaries. To the accompaniment of prayers and Bible-reading, small children had their heads banged on marker trees so that they would not forget where the boundaries lay. Such customs were carried to the United States by the early settlers. Ironically, the urban gangs of major US cities perpetuate these ancient pagan and Christian traditions when they spray graffiti onto walls in order to indicate the limits of "their" territory.

Similar boundary-marking rituals are to be found among traditional societies. The ceremonies of the Iraqw people of Tanzania are a good example. In their case a sheep or goat is taken to the limits of the territory and walked around the boundaries. When the marking has been affirmed in this way, the animal is suffocated. The body is cut into pieces which are subsequently distributed to various parts of the boundary. The three-day ritual is conducted by the leaders of the community, and it is regarded as achieving the purification and sanctific-ation of the homeland territory.

It is useful to distinguish between two basic types of human territory – primary and secondary territories.

Opposite
This aerial view of an Amazonian village in Brazil shows an arrangement of dwellings that provides for constant social interaction and communication. The wedge-shaped gardens in the circle are a focal point for tribal activity. Contrast this pattern with that found in the high-rise apartment blocks of New York (*left*). Here the design discourages group activity and the development of social relationships. Each set of occupants is isolated from the others.

Primary territories are those which belong exclusively to an individual or a small group. The family home is a classic example of such a territory: people from without the family do not enter unless specifically invited. Within the home, even further degrees of privacy and isolation may be available in individual rooms; for example, a teenager's bedroom may be forbidden territory to other family members. The personal nature of both houses and rooms is clearly evident in the way in which they are individually styled and decorated. If we look at a row of houses whose architecture is identical we almost always find that the occupants have painted their front door and other aspects of the façade in colours which contrast with their neighbours' décor in order to establish distinctiveness.

Primary territories provide people with an essential sense of security and they meet a universal need. On their home territories people tend to display dominance over others, while in someone else's primary space they show appropriate signs of deference and submission. In virtually all cultures, whether traditional or modern, individuals and families construct separate dwellings not just to meet the requirements of shelter and protection but also to create their own territorial integrity.

Secondary territories are less exclusive spaces. Nevertheless, they are central to people's lives and are of great importance because they facilitate patterns of regular collective interaction. In modern societies secondary territories may take the form of parks, squares, malls, neighbourhood bars and cafés, and that very special British social institution, the pub. In most cases, such territories invoke a sense of belonging and part-ownership in those people who use the places regularly. There may even be unofficial rules concerning special seats for individuals or particular privileges afforded to those of certain rank and status.

This kind of territory is likewise found all over the world. In tribal villages we find not only collections of huts and dwellings but also shared spaces in which social interaction between the occupants of the primary spaces takes place on a regular and sustained basis. There is, however, one territorial feature unique to modern societies: because it runs counter to the natural pattern of tribal living, it has created numerous problems. This special kind of territory consists of the entrance areas, hallways and corridors of apartment blocks.

The urban planner Oscar Newman, in his influential book *Defensible Space*, stressed the importance of these areas, which link the primary territory of the home to that of the public world. Where blocks are designed in such a way that the secondary areas are not felt to be within the jurisdiction of the occupants, vandalism and other crimes are commonplace. Entrances are often occupied by vagrants and alcoholics, and amenities such as elevators are constantly subject to criminal damage. Interactions taking place within such spaces are mostly impersonal, and even close neighbours may fail to greet each other.

Newman proposed that this state of affairs could be simply remedied through various design modifications. He suggested that proper control of these secondary territories can be established only when about 4–5 families share a single entrance; in such circumstances people get to know each other and take a strong interest in potential threats to their shared area. Subdivision of large blocks into units whose scale is more human radically alters the pattern of social behaviour.

What Newman proposed is, of course, a return to the use of collections of living areas which more closely resemble those found in traditional cultures. If we create units which do not have a human scale, we inevitably experience all the problems engendered by the dehumanization of the people using those units. The violence and alienation expressed in the inner-city areas of modern nations likewise serve to warn us that we have exceeded the limits set by our tribal heritage.

MYTHS AND RELIGIONS

All cultures subscribe to myths – stories which have no basis in truth or reality but which provide a rationale for religious beliefs and practices. The formal religious movements, which have varying degrees of power and influence in modern societies, are directly comparable to the systems of beliefs in spirits, gods and unseen spirits so characteristic of tribal societies. With typical ethnocentricity, we prefer to see our religions as qualitatively different from those of the African tribesman – somehow more divine, true and civilized. But this is a fallacy. When we attend church, pray to our God or perform sacred rituals, we are engaging in behaviours which are as old as human culture itself.

Myths serve a number of important functions in any society. To some extent they provide a history of a culture in the form of a narrative tale. Many myths refer to migrations, natural disasters, earlier forms of social organization, and significant leaders and heroes. Such histories, however, are rarely reliable because over long periods of time they become distorted beyond recognition. With cultural diffusion there is also the tendency to mix up stories – many simply apocryphal – originating from different societies. This applies as much to the Christian Bible, the Old Testament in particular, as to the folktales of preliterate cultures and the holy books of the other major religions.

The historical aspect of myths often includes an account of the origin of the universe itself. In the Judaeo-Christian tradition we find this in the book of *Genesis*, but it occurs also in many myths of tribal cultures. The anthropologist William Haviland provides us with an example of an origin myth from the Fon tribe of Dahomey, West Africa:

> In the beginning the stars were visible both at night and in the daytime. The night stars were the children of the moon and the day stars were the children of the sun. One day the moon told the sun that their children were trying to outshine them. To prevent this they agreed to tie up the stars in sacks and throw them in the ocean. The sun went first and cleared the daytime sky of stars. The sly moon, however, did not keep her part of the bargain, but kept all of her children in the night sky. The sun's children became all the brightly coloured fish in the ocean, and from that time the sun has been the mortal enemy of the moon, pursuing her to get revenge for the loss of the stars to the sea. When there is an eclipse, the sun is trying to eat up the moon.

Such a myth can be analysed in detail to provide an insight into the collective attitudes and values of the Fon. At a more simple level, it functions within the tribe as an explanation for several aspects of nature: the fish in the sea, the perceived rotation of the sun and moon around the sky, and those rare, but often frightening, eclipses.

A second major function of myths and religion is to provide a basis for law and morality. They have the effect of maintaining the status quo through reference to divine wishes and the sacred order of things. This is clear in all of the religious bibles, especially Judaism's Torah and Islam's Koran. Various groups in Western societies selectively draw on books of the Old Testament to justify their activities and to exert a controlling influence on their members. A notable example is the

Above
Funerals serve as occasions not only for the ritual expression of grief and mourning for the dead but also for the reaffirmation of social bonds between the living. The women in this Italian funeral procession are united by their publicly shared grief.

Right
In this New Guinea village tribal links with ancestors are maintained long after they are dead. Each year the mummified corpse of a long-deceased family member is brought out and sat on a chair. In front of him is placed the money that has been amassed during the past 12 months by his descendants – a kind of tribal stocktaking.

use of the epistles of Saint Paul to maintain gender roles and patterns of dominance in Christian cultures.

Another reason for myths is to provide answers to very basic questions which people in all cultures must ask. We need to understand the point of life itself, why we are here and what is our purpose. The formal religions of modern societies and the systems of ghosts and spirits in tribal cultures serve to allay such fundamental anxieties by providing easily understood notions of our earthly roles. For example, the belief in an afterlife, intrinsic to so many religions and myths, allows people to cope with the well founded fear of dying – the threat of nothingness.

If we accept that our religions are a continuance of mythical traditions established in earlier tribal societies, the individuals who hold authority in some areas of the modern sacred world can be seen in the same light as the shamans of traditional cultures. The shaman is a religious specialist who appears able to communicate directly with the spirit world, often through the induction of trance-like states. This role is nicely illustrated in the case of Inuit shamanism.

Inuit is the indigenous term for the people popularly known as the Eskimos. The shaman in this culture presides over the relationships between people and the supernatural beings who are thought to influence their lives. He is, therefore, involved in such activities as driving evil spirits away from the hunting fields in order to ensure a good supply of meat. He is the man to whom people turn when the sick need a cure, when the future must be foretold, and when good weather is essential for some important activity.

Part of the Inuit system of beliefs involves the notion that lack of fish in a particular area could be due to the anger of spirits such as the Sea-Woman. The anger might stem from the fact that someone had eaten a forbidden part of a fish, the offence caused by the action having soiled the Sea-Woman's hair. The role of the shaman in such an instance would be to contact the Sea-Woman in order to comb the dirt out of her hair and thus pacify her rage.

The general characteristic of shamans is that their authority is essentially charismatic. They are self-appointed and rely on their ability to sustain the group's belief in their powers and skills. In this and other senses they have much in common with the evangelists, faith healers, clairvoyants and straightforward magicians of Western cultures. The mystics of Asian cultures who have had such a profound influence in Britain and the United States, such as the Bhagwan and the Maharishi, are even closer to the shamans in concept, if not in style. However, even within the formal churches, despite their strenuous attempts to distance themselves from the mystical charlatans, elements of shamanism are clearly in evidence. The Christian priest called to exorcise the Devil from a troubled house has much in common with his Inuit counterpart.

2 RITES OF PASSAGE

TRADITIONAL RITES

In the large majority of traditional societies the transition from one level or status to another is marked by distinctive initiation ceremonies and rituals. Becoming a full member of a tribe, for example, with its associated rights and obligations, is not something which is achieved merely by coming of age. The transition from the status of child to that of adult is an event of such significance that it must be marked through traditional rites which clearly announce the new position of an individual within his (less frequently her) tribal group.

Rites of passage exist primarily to deal with what we might call "life crises". Birth, puberty, marriage, parenthood and death are all milestones in the "career" of the tribe member. The associated rituals not only mark the passing of such points, they also help to deal with the personal anxieties and stresses which such major life changes bring with them. In most cases the ceremonies have three distinct parts, as illustrated by the male initiation rites of Australian Aborigines.

The time for such initiation is decided by the elders, who have been watching the boy's progress through puberty. At this point begins the separation phase. The novice is taken from the village despite ritualized wailing by the women, who put up a show of physically resisting his removal. Once the boy is away from the tribe, the transition phase begins. Usually this involves some form of bodily mutilation, such as circumcision or the removal of teeth. These symbolic acts are thought by anthropologists to represent a "killing" of the initiate. He becomes "dead" to the normal life of his tribe.

In this isolated situation, which may last 6–8 weeks, the young boy is prepared for his later tribal role. He is given intensive training in the lore and ways of the tribe. In preliterate societies this is a useful mechanism for transmitting the culture from one generation to another, and its importance is highlighted by the degree of ritual which surrounds it. The initiate is also taught the art and cultural significance of tribal dancing, and shown those sites which are of special religious significance.

Eventually, the initiate returns to his village as a "man", and is greeted by the tribe as if he had returned from the dead. This symbolic death and rebirth emphasizes to the tribe his status as a new and quite different person, and henceforward all tribal members will behave towards him with due regard to the adult role he now plays.

The painful ordeals which the initiate has to bear, such as circumcision, have the clear function of binding him to his tribe. Through his suffering he declares his commitment and shows his courage. The more severe the ordeal, the greater the degree of solidarity engendered among fellow sufferers. This perhaps explains why many traditional societies put each of their individuals to the test on several occasions. Also in Australia, in the case of the Mardujara Aborigines, for example, circumcision is just one of the painful experiences through which the developing adolescent must pass. In early puberty his nasal septum is pierced with a small bone. His later circumcision is performed by two maternal uncles, in

isolation from the rest of the tribe. A year later, his penis is subjected to subincision, which involves making a lengthwise cut on its underside. Only after the scars of this final ceremony have healed is the young man allowed to marry. Even now, however, he is expected for a further decade to perform specific duties for his elders, such as providing them with meat.

Among the Gisu of Uganda, male circumcision plays an even more central role in the establishment of tribal bonding and identity; indeed, it is circumcision which, they believe, identifies them as a people quite distinct from their neighbouring cultures. The Gisu refer to themselves as "Basani", men, while other groups, because of their failure to circumcise, are lumped together under the label of "Basinde" – boys.

The Gisu circumcision ritual, known as Imbalu, reflects the cultural importance attached to the act. The young males, some as old as their early twenties, are required to show no fear and to remain perfectly still while the foreskin is cut away and flesh stripped from around the head of the penis. The initiate must be like the warrior who conquers his fear through the belief that he has the inner strengths and resources to succeed against his enemies.

The circumcision rites among the Papuans of New Guinea appear to be even more severe and demanding. The initial stages begin with fasting, followed by the ritual consumption of a dish consisting of nettles cooked in bamboo with pork fat. This produces a painful, stinging sensation followed by swelling of the throat. Two days later, nose bleeding is induced by hammering sharp pegs into the

The ceremony of the Habiye is held every year in Niamtougou in Toga and focuses on the exorcism of dead spirits. Death is symbolized by the Cincin snake, shown spiked on a stick, and by poisonous toads which are held in the mouth. During the ceremony, men wearing traditional costume and headdress mime the attributes of the animals they represent, and engage in dances that symbolize their supremacy over death. The snakes, toads and other symbols of evil are cut up, placed in cauldrons and taken in procession through the village. A second cauldron follows, filled with ashes, representing purity and life.

nostrils with wooden pounders. This is followed by cutting small wedges of flesh from around the glans penis, producing deep lacerations which often penetrate the urethra. As if this were not a sufficient ordeal for the initiate, the penis is now beaten repeatedly using the bamboo handle of the circumcision knife, and then rubbed vigorously with salt and nettles.

In some cases the preparations which take place prior to the more painful phases of the initiation ceremonies appear to induce a psychological state known as hyperaesthesia. This typically follows sustained fasting and lack of sleep, and is a phenomenon well known to interrogators and the agents of torture all around the world. The effect on the individual is to make him or her much more impressionable and susceptible to suggestion. All the messages communicated to a tribal member during the initiation rites are therefore likely to be indelibly imprinted, securing his undying commitment to the rules and traditions of the culture of which he proceeds to become a full member.

In traditional tribes, rites of initiation are almost always restricted to the males, and most of them involve mutilation of the penis, the most tender part of the male anatomy and, of course, the most visible sign of the individual's sexuality. From a Western point of view, such initiation rituals may seem barbaric and unnecessarily painful. The idea of inflicting deliberate pain and suffering on adolescents is one which would not be tolerated at an official level in modern societies. In recent times, the increasing levels of Western influence on some tribal societies have curtailed the more painful practices; for example, Australian Aborigines who have abandoned their traditional ways only rarely indulge in subincision. Yet to dismiss such rituals as "primitive" forms of barbarism is to ignore the vital role which they play in traditional cultures. Those societies which have ceased to engage in these practices have also lost much of the pattern of bonding and affiliation which previously secured their cultural and economic survival. When traditional rites of passage are discouraged, the entire social fabric starts to become unstitched.

The true role of tribal initiation rituals is highlighted also by the eagerness shown by the initiates. Far from being motivated to try to avoid the pain and suffering, boys and young men plead to be allowed the experience and the transitions which follow. For them it is an essential part of growing up and acquiring distinct status and identity. To be a full member of the tribe, with all its rights and obligations, is something for which a price must be paid, and this price is paid willingly.

MODERN RITES

There are, of course, many examples of rites of passage to be found in mainstream modern societies. Most religions provide for a pattern of orderly development and incorporation into the church. Baptisms and first communions are token rites in most Christian organizations. The Bar Mitzvah of Jewish culture is a more distinctive marking of the transition from boyhood to manhood, and circumcision is employed explicitly to indicate cultural membership. In other contexts, male circumcision is now performed ostensibly for reasons of health and hygiene.

However, it is in the fringe societies and sects present in modern cultures that tribal rites of passage are most clearly seen. Although they rarely involve the same degrees of physical mutilation and suffering as those found in traditional societies, they serve much the same function. They ensure obedience and

Above
A young woman of the Mehinacu tribe, Amazon, Brazil. As soon as girls begin to menstruate they are sent to separate huts for six months. The strings around the neck and the long fringes indicate their status prior to the initiation ceremony. They see only other women who visit with children during this period.

Opposite
Initiation of a young male in the Sudan. The painful incisions around the forehead must be endured without signs of physical distress or pain. When the wounds heal, they will leave behind the characteristic scars that identify the individual as a full adult member of his tribe.

conformity to group norms through creating a situation in which initiates are highly susceptible to persuasion.

Outside organized crime, the Freemasons are perhaps the best known example of a contemporary "secret society". Although claims have been made that the origins of the Freemason order can be traced back to the erection of the Tower of Babel, less fanciful evidence suggests that it had its roots in the guilds of masons and stonecutters in the 12th century. The tradition of secrecy probably arose from the artisans' desire to restrict knowledge concerning some of the more allegorical aspects of Gothic architecture and its symbolic details, as carved by the masons of the time. In addition, the use of special secret signs in the carvings served to identify the mason as a true craftsman rather than an imposter.

Modern Freemasonry was founded in 1717 with the establishment of the Grand Lodge of England, and since that time the order has gained substantial influence in all areas of the British establishment. Its durability and internal solidarity owe much to the seemingly archaic rituals in which nearly half a million men secretly take part at the monthly Lodge meetings. The most extreme rituals are reserved for the admission of new members who, while not subjected to physical torture, are made to engage in a form of behaviour which in any other setting would be considered ridiculous and demeaning.

The exact details of the initiation ceremony are still partly protected by the wall of secrecy which surrounds Freemasonry. The symbolic artifacts of such rituals, however, include ropes and daggers, white gloves, aprons and blindfolds. Words which have little meaning to outsiders, such as "Jahbulon", "Tubalcain" and "Boaz", are intoned by the assembled members as the initiate is made to roll up one trouser leg and, standing with a noose around his neck, to swear archaic oaths of allegiance. He is reminded all the time that the penalties should he reveal the secrets of the order involve tearing out his tongue and cutting his throat. In such an atmosphere of unreality and mysticism, commitment to this modern tribe is assured. How else could the new member justify the lengths to which he has gone in order to seek admittance? The ordeal is a psychological one, rather than a test of physical endurance or of tolerance to pain, but it appears to be every bit as effective.

The rewards for undergoing such rituals are considerable, which accounts for the initial motivation of so many members. The "brotherhood" includes many members of parliament, lawyers, doctors, architects and those in charge of public-works contracts. It also includes, to many people's consternation, a surprisingly high number of senior police officers and judges. To be initiated into this tribe is to improve one's chances of receiving assistance from people who are in positions of considerable power and influence.

Of course, Freemasonry is not the sole preserve of the British. It flourishes in France and other European countries, and there are a number of Lodges in the United States. There is also now in London a women's Freemason Lodge – a rather surprising institution considering that the order has traditionally been very much an all-male affair. The female Freemasons have adopted every detail of the rituals and traditions, even referring to themselves as "gentlemen". Their processes of initiation are much the same as those of their male counterparts, binding members together in tightly knit sorority.

The Freemasons are generally viewed as respectable members of the host cultures in which they flourish, although the secretive nature of their activities can sometimes be a cause of suspicion and distrust. A similar organization which

Opposite
In modern societies, mainstream rites of passage tend to lack the physical pain and suffering that characterizes their counterparts in traditional cultures. The collective celebration of the first communion, however, clearly marks a transition in status for members of Christian religious and social groups.

has shed some of its secretive cloak is the Rosicrucian order. This is one of a number of contemporary organizations purporting to possess secrets which can magically transform the lives of all who become members. Advertisements in national newspapers still subtly hint at the potential for self-fulfilment and access to undreamed success and riches. Founded on a mixture of alchemy and Christianity, the original Rose Cross Brotherhood was a secret organization whose ostensible function was to cure the sick and put the considerable magical talents of its members to positive use in the community. The modern fraternity is less a continuance of the tradition than an attempt to recreate it: AMORC (Ancient and Mystic Order Rosae Crucis), the California-based body responsible for the newspaper advertisements was founded as recently as 1916. It claims to seek to restore the lost arts and to provide influential men with skills to rule the world in an orderly and productive fashion.

The attractions of such a doctrine are considerable. Many underachievers have been drawn by the promise of self-enrichment through access to secret teachings. Although the true nature of the contemporary Rosicrucian orders is a little unclear, it is probable that some elements of the traditional initiation ceremonies have been retained. Although the details of such rites have changed over the centuries, they have always included elements similar in character to those found in the Freemason ceremonies. In some ceremonies initiates had their hands bound and a noose placed around their neck. Accompanied by their sponsors, they were obliged to swear oaths of allegiance in order that the symbolic threat of strangulation be removed and their admission to the circle of the brotherhood be effected. Access to the real secrets, however, came much

Opposite
Group exposure to ordeals unites those who take part because of their collective suffering. Here Japanese men take an ice-bath in midwinter at the Teppozu Inari Shrine in Tokyo.

Below
An Australian Aborigine boy undergoes the painful ordeal of circumcision, which is carried out by his uncles and other male relations. Similar initiation rituals are to be found all over the world, and male circumcision is, of course, a central feature of modern Judaism.

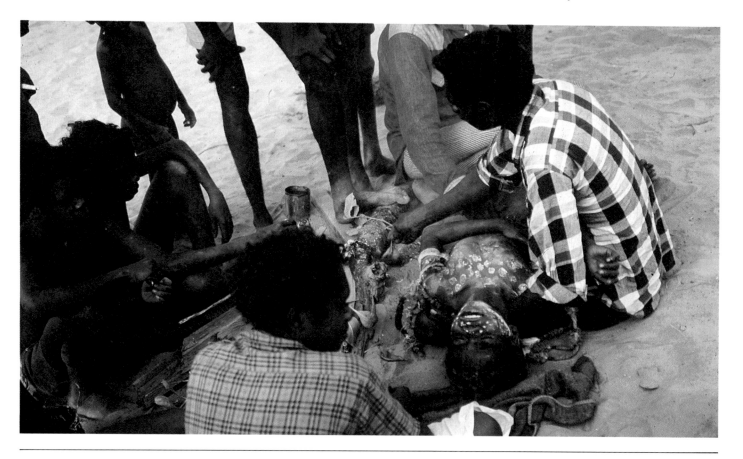

later, after further stages of initiation and transition to the higher orders, or "degrees", had been completed.

The importance of rites of passage as a way of ensuring individuals' loyalties to their modern tribe can best be seen in the example of the Church of Scientology, invented by the science-fiction writer L. Ron Hubbard. The story goes that Hubbard created this organization purely in response to a bet in a bar that he could not devise an enduring new religion. Scientology is based on the amateur form of psychoanalysis which he had earlier invented, Dianetics, and most of its tenets are not of interest here. However, what Hubbard built into the structure of the church was a ladder of rites of passage: in order to attain complete psychological self-realization, the Scientologist must graduate to progressively higher ranks, the criterion of graduation being essentially the passing of an examination. What ties the individual to the Scientology tribe, however, is not so much the kudos of holding high rank but the fact that, in order to achieve each new rung on the status ladder, he or she must spend a fairly large sum of money: in this case the pain of the rite of passage is financial rather than physical. Of course, once a person has invested so much in the attainment of high rank, the temptation to leave the church is minimized; indeed, there is every incentive to expend yet more money to travel further up the ladder. (In addition, dire penalties – such as total ostracism from one's Scientological friends – are threatened should individuals nevertheless decide to opt out completely.)

A similar effect is to be found among devotees of fantasy role-playing games. As with Scientology, the aim of the player is to accumulate status – in this case in the form of an increased number of "hit points", "magical powers", or whatever. Of course, these qualifications are of relevance only in terms of the game; yet they are important to the individual in the eyes of his or her peers. Once one has attained a certain level of status, one must expend more money in order to advance further, perhaps by buying an additional boxful of rules and equipment. These games are largely played by adolescents, who usually have to make quite considerable sacrifices in order to afford each new "rite of passage". Yet individuals are perfectly happy to make those sacrifices: they have spent a good deal of money achieving their current status, so further expenditure and its reward, still higher status, provide a more appealing option than simply "throwing it all away".

While the "magical" rites of Freemasons, Rosicrucians and a host of similar organizations may seem to outsiders a little bizarre, as do the tenets of Scientology and role-playing games, most of us blithely accept the less ostentatious and dramatic forms of initiation to be found in more familiar settings. Those little promises uttered by Boy Scouts and Girl Guides may seem far removed from the ordeals of tribal warriors, but their function is exactly the same. Similarly, the freshman at Oxford University sits through a matriculation ceremony, incomprehensible to those not fluent in Latin, in order that he or she can be incorporated into the lower ranks of a very special academic tribe.

MASCULINE ORDEALS

In contrast to purely symbolic rites, initiation rituals of a more physical nature are still encountered in modern societies, most frequently all-male institutions. Boys' boarding schools and army regiments are typical examples.

The tradition in many British schools, despite the influence of progressive education and changing official attitudes towards physical violence, is to subject new boys to a variety of forms of humiliation and painful ordeal. Old boys of such schools look back with wistful nostalgia to their initiation experiences, using phrases such as "character building", "loyalty" and "being a man". While the practices may now be less common – even the headmaster of Eton reports that boys in his school are today much nicer to each other – they still continue and still serve the same function.

Typical schoolboy initiation rituals revolve around the novice's transition through adolescence. His testicles may be smeared with boot polish or his first pubic hairs may be shaved off. "Debagging", whereby the individual's trousers are removed in order to reveal his genitalia, is a milder practice which few males who have been to single-sex schools have managed to escape. The ritual floggings of the new boys, so vividly depicted in *Tom Brown's Schooldays*, are now thought to have disappeared completely. In the modern armed forces, however, high levels of brutality in initiation ceremonies are not at all uncommon.

A recent exposé of life in the British Army's Coldstream Guards has revealed the kinds of ritual violence to which new recruits are subjected. In one case a novice had his testicles burned with a blowtorch. He was also wrapped in a mattress and, after being repeatedly kicked, was dropped out of a window onto the ground $4\frac{1}{2}$ m (15 ft) below. Some recruits have been sodomistically raped, and others forced to drink urine. Ex-members of other regiments have reported

Obedience to legitimate authority is a central feature of tribal groups. In modern armies this is developed to an extreme extent. Through the suppression of individuality and the fostering of group loyalties, officers ensure that their messages reach a receptive audience.

Pages 44-5
The annual Football Association Cup Final at Wembley is the pinnacle of the English soccer season – an occasion for elaborate displays of tribal loyalties among the fans on the terraces. Within the seemingly disorderly patterns of behaviour often witnessed at soccer matches exists a very distinct social order, characterized by hierarchies, role positions and social rules.

similar rituals, and it is clear that there have been occasions on which quite serious injuries have been sustained.

Media reaction to those who have made known the details of these initiation ceremonies has been mixed. Some people have argued that an immediate stop must be made to these "degrading" and dangerous practices. They protest that, in the army as outside it, quasi-legalized assaults of this kind should not be tolerated. Others, in stark contrast, view the people who have "ratted" on their comrades as "cowards" and "wimps". Being a man, they proclaim, means being able to take your punishment without running for help to the authorities. If you cannot stand a little manly "fun", then the army is no place for you.

Such differences in sentiment reflect the increasing ambivalence in Western societies toward not only the violent aspects of initiation rituals but also the concepts of tribalism and bonding themselves. To describe a group as "cliquish" or "insular" is to make an essentially pejorative remark. The fact that a group achieves a high degree of collective identity through traditional forms of incorporation of new members is seen as alarming to those outside that group. Yet it is partly because distinctive markings of transition from one level of status to another are largely lacking in mainstream modern cultures that so many people are confused about the role they are expected to play. The "trauma" of adolescence, for example, is as much due to the state of limbo which exists between the role of child and that of adult as it is to the rapid development of sexual maturity.

For males, adolescence is a period marked by dramatically increased production of the hormone testosterone. This is the chemical which is responsible for the enlargement of the testes and the development of secondary sexual characteristics, such as pubic and facial hair. The other effects of testosterone, however, include in most cases an increased aggressiveness. It is possible initiation rituals, related as they usually are to the onset of puberty, developed and survived because they were effective in controlling this new-found energy and in directing it into socially acceptable activities. Using such a procedure, tribal elders could tame the potential for rebellion among the younger members and secure their loyalty and obedience.

In most modern cultures such suppression of youthful vigour and questioning would seem very out of place. But, while seemingly cruel rituals have largely vanished from mainstream cultures, little has been provided in their place. In the face of this lack of direction and means of affiliation, forms of initiation have developed in subcultural contexts. The fraternities and sororities of universities in the United States, for example, highlight people's need for tribal bonds at a critical time of life, and initiation into such closed societies is, for many students, the most significant of their college experiences.

YOUTH GANGS

Some youth cultures have evolved their own initiation rites – although we should note at the outset that these are often surrounded by myths generated by prurient media interest. In US street gangs potential new members are sometimes required to show what they are made of before they are admitted to the tribe. Often the requirements amount to no more than the commission of a fairly minor criminal offence. In this way the new recruit is bound to the group through his shared complicity in illegal activities. In other cases he will be admitted as a "brother" only after his blood has been mingled with that of his fellows. This usually involves making minor cuts to the hand, but the symbolic significance is quite considerable. Hell's Angels are reputed to have more dramatic initiation ceremonies, involving such acts as biting the heads off live pigeons or chickens.

These are, however, exceptions to a general rule. In most cases young people attach themselves to a subculture simply by dressing in appropriate ways, adopting prescribed patterns of adornment and subscribing actively to the values, attitudes and general style which characterize the tribe's distinctiveness. Nevertheless, although they avoid the rigours of initiation, youth cultures provide for orderly transition and the achievement of status within their alternative social framework. This sense of "career" structure is particularly apparent in the British football subculture and in the street gangs of the United States.

British football-fan tribes share some common elements with youth gangs in the United States. The football culture provides an umbrella framework for the various groups of supporters of particular teams. Football fans, whether from Liverpool, Birmingham or anywhere else, have similar styles of dress and behaviour and subscribe to the same general set of values and attitudes. Each particular tribe, however, comes into conflict from time to time with the others it encounters when two teams meet on the football field. Similarly, US youth gangs share a common cultural framework, but each defends its own territory with considerable aggressive determination.

The youth gang is organized in a clearly hierarchical way, with formal titles for members – President, Vice-President, Armourer, and so on down the line. The football-fan tribe is much more loosely structured, partly because its members usually meet only once a week in the ceremonial territories of the football terraces. However, closer inspection reveals a distinctive social network, with three main tiers based around age sets.

Football fans tend to enter this alternative culture at an age of about 9–11. Being small, these children occupy the front parts of the terracing behind the goals, where their view of the game is not obscured by others in the crowd. Yet the progress of the game is often not their primary concern: for much of the time they can be seen facing back toward the upper terraces, closely observing the activities of the older boys behind them.

These "novices" in the fan tribe are engaged in a process of social learning, acquiring knowledge of the ritual chants and songs and the occasions on which it is appropriate to use them. Their style of non-verbal behaviour, including posture, facial expressions and gestures, gradually changes in response to the influences around them. Moreover, they begin to internalize the various attitudes and ideas expressed by their older role-models.

This "novice" period lasts for up to 3–4 years, its end being marked by a sudden shift of position on the terraces and incorporation into the main body of vociferous fans. This usually happens at the beginning of a new football season, and thus marks a distinct transition from the status of "little kid" to that of "one of the boys". The main group which they have joined is essentially the core of the soccer culture. The individuals involved are commonly referred to as "thugs", "savages" or "mindless hooligans" in the popular media. A more neutral term to describe them is Rowdies, for this more accurately describes their routine patterns of behaviour.

Being accepted as a Rowdy represents a second tier within the tribe. It involves constant displays of loyalty and commitment to the team which the tribe supports. The opposing fans are required to be ritually denigrated and certain standards of courage, or "bottle", are expected. A Rowdy should not run from encounters with rivals, but neither should he act in such a way as to attract the attentions of the police or incite levels of violence which result in serious injury. To aid his sense of career development, a number of informal role positions are available to which he might aspire.

Most tribes of football fans have identifiable, although not formally selected, leaders whose functions vary considerably. There are Chant Leaders whose task is to initiate singing and chanting at appropriate points throughout the match. This might sound relatively easy, but there are certain hazardous features in the enactment of this role. If a fan raises his arms and shouts out the first few words of a chant, but finds that nobody else is prepared to join in with him, then distinct loss of face results. The Chant Leader must therefore have the confidence of those around him and understand the subtle rules governing the use of chants.

Aggro Leaders are those who initiate fighting in and around the football grounds. Their role within the grounds is now quite limited, due to the installation of various security measures, but opportunities arise for minor skirmishes outside the ground and on journeys to matches away from home. The nature of the violence in which they are involved, however, has particular tribal features which render conflicts relatively bloodless, as discussed in Chapter 10.

Other recognizable roles include various kinds of Organizers. These fans are responsible for coordinating travel to away matches, liaising with club officials, disseminating information and generally helping to maintain group cohesion. A particularly interesting position, however, is that of the Nutter (or Headbanger). Nutters are individuals with a reputation for being quite mad and doing things which no sane fan would ever do. They are deviants within their own culture, but their presence is tolerated because they serve a useful function. By breaking the unstated rules of the tribe, they remind others of what the rules really are. Also, like officially tolerated jesters and clowns, they provide amusement. While they can sometimes be a danger to themselves and their group by, for example, issuing challenges to large groups of rivals, they are usually prevented by their fellow tribe members from going too far.

It is in the Rowdies status-level that a fan's tribal activities are at their most intense. Like his counterpart in traditional African culture, it is at this stage that his displays of warrior potential and his wearing of the tribal dress and insignia will be most marked. Such constant symbols of commitment and loyalty, however, are difficult to maintain over a long period: there are, after all, other considerations which he has to keep in mind, such as finding and retaining a regular job and getting married. An additional problem is that routine fan activity brings those involved to the attention of the police, who are generally keen to put an end to their rituals. For these reasons, a further stage of transition – the third tier – is provided within the football culture. Once an individual's reputation has been firmly established, he can safely abandon some of the more onerous requirements and become a Graduate.

To talk of football fans graduating may seem a little odd, but the term is very appropriate. They have done the equivalent of attending lectures and writing essays. They have been examined by their peers and elders, and now they rest on their laurels. They remain, however, firmly within the tribe, taking on a role of sage-like aloofness, but coupled with this is an unchallenged sense of commitment and influence. They rarely engage in the chants and the issuing of ritual insults and challenges; such things they leave to the young warriors. They may even stand in a part of the ground not specifically designated as part of their tribe's home territory. Yet, like the elders of traditional tribes, they are the guardians of their culture.

Patterns of transition like those of the football tribes are found in other youth cultures. There are few specific rites and the rules are rarely formulated in any fixed way, but the basic process is very much in evidence, providing for those who seek the special rewards of tribal bonding a sense of true worth through progression and the attainment of status in the eyes of their peers.

In formally constituted associations the points of transition are more clearly marked. In the Boy Scouts and Girl Guides, for example, we find both age-set distinctions and status-linked career points. The transition from being a Cub to being a Scout takes place at a particular age. A number of role positions are then available – for example, Patrol Leader – and marks of respect, in the form of badges and insignia, are bestowed on those who achieve particular distinction. The part played by individuals in the rituals of these two tribes varies with their position, much as it would in a traditional culture. The camp-fire ceremonies symbolize a desire to return to an earlier pattern of life in which status is displayed and respect is marked.

In adult tribes, transition rites are often marked by special presentations or by elevation to special positions. Even the humblest flower-arranging society creates a social structure in which the part played by each member can be clearly delineated and defined. These mini-bureaucracies reinforce collective identity through giving the tribe structure and through allowing individual identities to be created within it. Thus the presentation of the Oscars and the creation of a new British Peer of the Realm are equally, and equivalently, manifestations of tribal behaviour.

3 EMBLEMS OF ALLEGIANCE

TRADITIONAL CLOTHING

In modern societies the "traditional" or "folk" forms of dress are rarely seen in an everyday context. They are displayed at so-called cultural festivals and on special anniversaries, so that spectators can enjoy a sense of nostalgia and collective heritage. More often, though, they are (usually inaccurately) run up to attract the tourists. Local plumbers and shop assistants don ill-fitting lederhosen and slap their thighs in discos at Austrian package-tour ski resorts. At Flamenco evenings on the Costa del Sol a pastiche of traditional costumes is presented to sunburned tourists drinking British beer. Perhaps at a tea ceremony in the hills above Tokyo one can begin to appreciate the real nature of an indigenous and meaningful form of dress in its true setting, but such opportunities are rare.

Traditional costume marked a person out as belonging to a discrete cultural unit, and often indicated his or her standing within that community. Such clothing provided far more than protection against the excesses of cold and heat, rain and wind. In terms of its design, its function as a means of ensuring a degree of modesty, through the masking of sexual signals, was relatively minor. Its main role was communication: the signalling of tribal affiliation.

Right
Sorority is eloquently expressed by girls in this tribal dance in Brazil, which is in celebration and remembrance of the women of the Amazon.

Opposite
Two little girls and a boy in Nambicuara prepare for their roles in later life. Although the boy is the youngest, he wears the chief's headdress and expects submissive attention from his female peers.

Large-scale religious organizations in modern societies employ dress and ceremonial clothing for expressive purposes in much the same way as members of traditional, tribal cultures – as seen here during a visit by Pope John Paul II to New Guinea.

In traditional cultures, especially those in subtropical regions, everyday clothing is often minimal; tribal affiliations are most commonly indicated through bodily decoration and disfigurement. But it is rare to find a tribe which does not have its own characteristic headdress or distinctive ceremonial costume. The fast-disappearing Bushmen of the Kalahari Desert in southwest Africa wear little more than leather loincloths and capes yet, despite their harsh life – they are often referred to as the most "primitive" culture in the world – they use culturally specific combinations of ostrich-shell beads carefully strung from tufts of hair and in characteristic bands around the arms and ankles.

Among the Dani of New Guinea, where clothing is similarly rudimentary, male decorative wear consists primarily of special feathers and cowrie shells. Considerable time is spent in preparing these elements of dress, although the final effect is often quite modest, lacking the elaborateness characteristic of, say, the distinctive headdresses of some traditional North American Indian cultures. Among Dani men, high status and decoration have an inverse relationship, with the most influential figures wearing little more than grass bracelets and neckbands. Power is signalled by the fact that an individual no longer needs to impress his peers through the means of decorative display. Outsiders, used to a more orthodox connection between dress and authority, might be confused by this subtle display rule; nevertheless, the Dani employ a medium of expression which is quite universal – that the degree of ostentation of dress reflects the

individual's status within the tribe. In the case of the Dani, it is merely that simpler dress implies higher status, rather than the other way around.

In tribal cultures which dwell in areas where climate dictates the wearing of more than simple protectors of modesty, opportunities arise for far more significant clothing displays. Although the descendants of the once proud and powerful Incas of South America are now largely reduced to subsistence farming and herding in the inhospitable Andes, they still cling to their traditional ways of producing intricately woven shawls, embroidered ponchos and knitted caps. These designs, which are thousands of years old, are now one of the few ways whereby the Incas can retain a significant part of their cultural heritage.

The Tuareg people were originally nomadic inhabitants of the central and southern Sahara, but now they live mainly settled lives in the Sudan and elsewhere on the fringes of the desert. A white-skinned race descended from the Berbers, they have a dress which is particularly striking and which still survives despite the inevitable forces of acculturation. The *litham* of the man consists of 3m (10ft) of cloth wound around the face and head to produce a combined turban and veil. While it may provide welcome protection from the sun's rays and from wind-blown sand, it serves also as both a clear tribal identifier and an indicator of status and maturity. Women and youths are not allowed to wear the *litham*. Adult men of higher status wear a black or indigo *litham*, while those of lesser social standing wear a white, undecorated version.

The cultural importance of a similar piece of headwear, the Sikh turban, is well illustrated in its continued use by Punjabi immigrants to countries of the West. This simple piece of clothing has such symbolic significance that Sikhs in Britain protested vehemently when a law was introduced to compel motorcyclists to wear crash helmets. A Sikh could not wear a helmet and a turban simultaneously and so, it was argued, the law was racially discriminatory. Sikhs contended that the wearing of this headdress was fundamental to their religion, but really the cause of their distress went deeper than that: as we have seen, religious doctrine is often central to the maintenance of tribal bonds and identity.

Religious dictates similarly constitute the ostensible rationale for the distinctive apparel of Hasidic Jews. Irrespective of the climate or the country in which they reside, the Hasidim adhere to the same costume. Whether in Brooklyn, Amsterdam or Tel Aviv, traditional black dresses are worn by the women while the men are never seen without their greatcoats and *streiml* hats; the males most closely associated with Rabbinical influence display their status by use of a fur band around the hat. Ironically, this style of dress is far from ancient: it is based on that worn in 18th-century Poland, whence many Hasidim originated. The function of the style of dress is not to ensure conformity with Talmudic law but to provide a sometimes incongruous statement of membership of a cultural unit.

Another form of ostensibly traditional tribal dress which has relatively modern aspects is the Scottish kilt. The *feilidh beag* skirt-like dress of Highland men dates back no further than the early 18th century. Before about 1725 the more

Above
The bonds and solidarity among Orthodox Jewish men are expressed through the traditional beards and style of dress which immediately identify their religious and cultural affiliations.

Opposite
Traditional lithams, seen here worn by Tuareg men.

affluent Scots wore belted trousers or breeches, while the poor were content with shirts of sufficient length to cover at least the upper parts of the legs.

The tartan, much revered by those of Highland descent, is of even more recent origin. We know that cloths of a woven plaid design were worn by the Scots at least as far back as 1440, but they were not originally designed to distinguish members of different clans. For example, in historical accounts of the Battle of Culloden, 1745, we find no reference to any distinguishing tartans, clan allegiances being detectable only by the colour and pattern of a man's bonnet.

It was not until toward the end of the 18th century that the tartans began to take on any heraldic significance. The design and colour of the cloths became standardized, eventually to provide the basis for clan insignia. Yet it is to these relatively modern tribal identifiers that descendants of the Scots cling in nostalgic attempts to prove their cultural heritage. Scottish expatriates in Bombay don the colours of the Campbells, Macdonalds, Frasers and Robertsons at Hogmanay in the grand Taj Hotel, in passionate demonstrations of cultural identity. Burns' night in cities as diverse as New York and Melbourne provides a further opportunity for the wearing of the hallowed cloths.

MODERN CLOTHING

The principle that dress and costume provide signals of tribal allegiance is easily demonstrated where there are clear ethnic/religious origins. But what of people

The "uniform" of the Amish is a simple puritan style of dress which seems out of keeping in today's United States. Its function is to reinforce ties among members of the communities and to signal their subscription to a distinct set of values.

Left
Middle-class women in unmistakeable style at Derby Day 1985 in England.

Below
The relatively modern kilts of the Scots worn by pipers at a Highland Games.

who consider themselves to be members of mainstream modern societies? To what extent do their clothes and stylistic accoutrements announce their tribal affiliations and declare their social identity?

The author Deyan Sudjic, in his entertaining book *Cult Objects*, sums up very crisply the true role that clothes play in modern societies:

> Not only are clothes intended to display wealth and status, but they are also tribal: they are there to give us a sense of belonging, or possibly more important on some occasions, of not belonging. That is as true of the bespoke city type with turnups and a detachable collar, as it is of the South London teenager in imported Italian sportswear that is far too expensive ever to risk on a playing field, but which does come in vivid easily identifiable colours. It is designed according to strict principles of legibility: the right number of stripes up each trouser leg; crests on polo shirts; and names on running shoes. The two groups may not have much else in common, but they are both using clothes to put across a particular message about themselves. And it is cult objects, such as the trenchcoat, which form the basis of the means by which the message is expressed.

In most cases fashion and ephemeral notions of style dictate the range of acceptable forms of clothing. But, within that range, each individual makes deliberate choices. By selecting a particular jacket or dress, people make a quite specific statement about themselves. They declare themselves as individuals, but they simultaneously indicate the extent to which they belong with other sets of individuals. Everyday clothes are, in a very real sense, distinctive uniforms conveying to other people important messages about the identity of the wearer.

Nowhere is this more true than in the formal world of business and high finance. The traditional English bowler hat of the "city gent" may now be in decline, but his dark suit, highly polished shoes, sober shirt and school tie are still unmistakable emblems. He is an elder of the City tribe – a tribe which travels

Contrasting styles of traditional dress, perhaps reflecting the varying roles which they play within their cultures. *Above*, Guatemalan village women and (*opposite*) the almost entirely masked bodies and faces of Iranian Chadored women.

daily to the modern equivalent of the hunting grounds, the financial institutions in the City of London's hallowed Square Mile. His rank as an elder is discernible because of the contrast between his style of dress and that of his younger rivals. The new breed of British super-rich wheeler-dealers declare their niche in the new computerized Stock Market by wearing clothes which are at once in keeping with their sober and responsible business while at the same time reflecting their youthful affluence and reputation for high living. The suits are lighter and more narrowly tailored, the shoes are by Gucci, and the ties are silk; all in all, the apparel nicely matches the Porsches and BMWs which are the other emblems of this modern tribe. A similar pattern is to be found in most of the other capital cities of the world. The details of the business dress style may differ, depending to some extent on climate and national temperament, but the uniforms can quickly be identified whether in Tokyo or Buenos Aires or on New York's Wall Street.

Identifiable uniforms are equally in evidence in other professions. Within the academic tribes of most modern societies great efforts are made to acquire just the right degree of affected scruffiness. To dress smartly and expensively is to be in breach of one of the unwritten tribal rules, which says that you cannot be a serious intellectual if you wear a Pierre Cardin suit. A tweed jacket, preferably with leather elbow patches, is much more likely to be in line. Even in the United States, where academics are less ashamed of making money than in other countries, professors of both sexes are usually ill at ease if dressed to a level of fashionable elegance which their financial peers would take for granted. The same sort of inverted relationship between success and standard of dress is noticeable in some of the professions, notably publishing.

Left
School sports days are welcome opportunities for boys to express their tribal loyalties, as manifested in the collective support of representatives in the races. Their simple uniform likewise reinforces their sense of being in a discrete social group.

Businessmen and academics, of course, belong to rather diffuse tribes, which is why we might sometimes fail to recognize them immediately from their style of dress alone. Where modern tribal groups are more closely knit, however, the uniformity of dress among the members becomes much more striking. The British upper classes at play are as recognizable as uniformed policemen. Observe the straw boaters and striped blazers at Henley Regatta: the ceremonial regalia of the privileged caste are every bit as much an emblem of power and authority as the symbolic dress of an African chieftain.

YOUTH CULTURE DRESS

In youth subcultures the meaning of dress becomes even more specific, even though the messages may not always be interpretable to "outsiders" from the mainstream host culture. Hell's Angels, for example, in both Britain and the United States not only adopt a style of dress which clearly identifies them as such but also decorate their clothes with symbols intelligible only to fellow tribe members. The style consists of denim Levi jackets with the arms removed and jeans with the bottoms cut off. On the back of the jackets are sewn the "colours", cloth badges bearing the legend "Hell's Angels" and, beneath, the name of the particular chapter to which the individual belongs. Other insignia include studs, Iron Crosses, swastikas and similar "shocking" emblems.

This basic style is instantly recognizable and, when coupled with the presence of Harley Davidson bikes, can be quite intimidating to "outsiders". Other details on the clothing, however, are less decipherable. A badge which simply says "SFFH" or "13" communicates little to those without specific knowledge of tribal

Opposite
Today, Royal Ascot, in England, has less to do with horse-racing than with ostentatious displays of upper-class style, as shown here in the wearing of bonnets.

Above
The standard uniform of the London City Gent.

Right
This North American Indian lawyer manages to signal his allegiances to both modern society and his tribal roots in the manner in which he dresses and plaits his hair.

lore. In fact, "SFFH" stands for "stoned forever, forever happy", while the number 13 represents the 13th letter of the alphabet, "M", representing the word "marijuana". Of even greater apparent obscurity is the badge that simply says "1%": this is a reference to a statement made in the 1960s by the American Motorcycle Association that 99 per cent of motorcyclists were decent, clean-driving young men.

This combination in dress style of starkly communicative elements with enigmatic details is a hallmark of tribal costume. First, it immediately identifies the clan allegiance of the wearer. Second, it strengthens his bonds with other members of the collective by indicating his access to shared meanings unknown to outsiders. The individual Hell's Angel wants to shock, outrage, and demonstrate his aggressive potential to "outsiders", but even more importantly he wants to be "one of the boys".

US street gangs share some of the stylistic leanings of the Hell's Angels. In New York, as in most major US cities, street gangs with impressive names such as "Crazy Homicides", "Montauk Chestbreakers" and "Savage Riders" vary in the precise details of their "colours", but all are recognizable as gang members. The uniform usually consists of sawn-off denim or leather jackets, often studded, carrying the gang's name and logo. The intricacy of these designs varies, the "classiest" of the gangs having them commercially embroidered. Bandannas tied

Traditional costume in Herero, South West Africa, is worn mainly by the women. The men tend to opt for a more Western style, which they feel enhances their status.

Young aspirants in the English youth culture. Known as ''Rudies'', these three boys, aged between 10 and 13, indicate their allegiances most specifically by their pork-pie hats.

around the head are commonplace, especially among Hispanic gang members, and heavy boots are part of the standard kit.

To be an active gang member is to belong to a tribe which takes pride in its potential for warfare. Most gangs actually have a designated Warlord, whose task it is to arrange orderly battles with rival gangs. The tribal costume reflects the warrior-like qualities in a number of ways. Leather cuffs with metal studs filed to sharp points endow the wearer with a hostile image, as do metal chains hanging from the belt. To wear such regalia is, of course, to invite the interest of the police, but that is a price most gang members are prepared to pay in their pursuit of a social identity in a world that has largely abandoned them.

Compared with the Hell's Angels and the ''Crazy Homicides'', the average British football fan presents himself as a quite unremarkable youth whose clothing is often not particularly distinctive. Nevertheless, it does include elements that have symbolic meaning. Analysis of the reactions of fans to individuals wearing various combinations of clothing items has shown that two distinct types of message are communicated by them. First, there is the toughness, or macho, signal; a combination of heavy Dr Marten boots (now less popular than in the 1970s) and a thin shirt worn in the middle of winter might be interpreted in this way. A cut-down denim jacket might also add a little to the aggressive image. The second principal message is, however, one of loyalty to the team which the individual supports, and hence to the particular terrace tribe associated with it. Note is taken of the wearing of team scarfs, especially if they are donned in unorthodox positions, such as around the wrist, so that there is no question of them being worn for the sake of warmth or comfort. Flags embellished with the team's insignia and worn around the shoulders, rather than waved, are likewise seen as tokens of loyalty and commitment.

Many social scientists regard these symbolic features of tribal dress as quite arbitrary. So long as all the members understand the significance of certain forms of clothing, then it hardly matters which are the specific elements used. This view, however, ignores some very striking historical parallels to the modern football-fan costume. Some 2000 years ago, in the hippodromes of the Roman Empire, vociferous tribal followers of chariot-racing teams displayed their devotions in much the same way as do contemporary British soccer supporters. In the 1st century AD Pliny the Younger, in a letter to a friend, showed a typical intellectual's misunderstanding of tribal activity but at the same time highlighted the role that dress played in this particularly striking example of group bonding. Describing the chariot races in the Circus Maximus, he commented:

> There is nothing new, no variety, nothing for which once is not enough. This makes me all the more surprised that so many thousands of grown men are prepared to see over and over again in such childish fashion galloping horses and men driving the chariots. If they were attracted by the horses' speed or the drivers' skill, there might be some sense in it. But as it is they merely support a piece of cloth; that is what they follow, and if the two colours were changed over in the middle of the race their support and allegiance would change too. . . . Fancy such influence and power wielded by one worthless shirt, not merely among the common crowd, which is even more worthless than that, but even among some men of taste.

The "worthless shirt" was, in fact, the essential token of membership of one of the circus factions. The major chariot teams rode in particular colours, the Blues

Opposite above and above
Bikers at the annual rally in Black Hills,
South Dakota. The pins and badges affixed to
the jackets have special significance within
the biker culture. Although Hell's Angels are
the most widely known of all motorcycle
subcultures, even Christians find a place
among the tribal worship of the motorcycle.

Right
The annual Henley Regatta provides the
setting for reunions of English upper-class
"Hooray Henries", who indicate their
privileged status through blazers, boaters
and other tribal insignia.

and the Greens being the most dominant. Their supporters identified with a particular team by wearing simple tunics of the appropriate colour. On circus days they must have presented a spectacle very much like the one we see at soccer cup finals at Wembley, although their numbers would have been twice as great. The tunics were designed with a wrist band on the end of the sleeves. As the arms were raised in salute the colours would also have been displayed in a manner very reminiscent of the effect achieved using football scarves knotted around the wrist. The football fan today employs a medium of tribal expression which has a heritage dating back far beyond the emergence of post-war British youth culture.

Tribal uniforms of other contemporary youth cultures, while lacking direct equivalents in earlier historical periods, are no less effective in their communication of social identity. In Britain, individuals have enjoyed opportunities to adopt the dress and customs of a variety of subcultural groups, the style of clothing reflecting the values and customs of the particular tribe. In the 1950s Teddy Boys posed in long jackets and suede shoes, looking suitably macho to the background strains of Bill Haley and His Comets. Some Teds subsequently modified their image slightly to become Rockabilly Rebels, or Rockers. Meanwhile, other teenagers seeking a source of tribal identity became Mods: their characteristic uniform consisted of a Parka anorak with red, white and blue target emblems on the back. Middle-class youth, by contrast, rejected the neat dress style of their mainstream contemporaries and frayed the ends of their bell-bottom jeans, donned fishermen's smocks and denim caps and paraded as Beatniks – the fashion of the disaffected drop-out. During the 1960s young people in California likewise dropped out, becoming Hippies, and their gaudy style spread among young people throughout the Western cultures. The Hippy "look" now serves as a metaphor for that entire decade.

Since then the British have had to grow accustomed not only to the overtly aggressive Skinheads, many of whom were involved in the establishment of the first football-hooligan clans during the mid-1960s, but also to the much more spectacularly dressed Punks, who appeared on the scene in the late 1970s. Some Skinheads, feeling that their tribe had lost its distinctiveness, smartened themselves up, put on pork-pie hats and became Rudies. Mods and Teds reappeared, fired with revivalist fervour. Some Punks, content with the expressive blackness of their uniform but ill at ease with all the razorblade earrings and nasal studs, underwent a subtle metamorphosis to be reborn as the slightly quieter Gothics.

It may seem that we have been concentrating excessively on British youth tribes, but in a very real sense they have set the style for many European emulators. The Raggare in Sweden may still see the Californian Hot Rodders as their role models, but French and German youth look to their peers in London for sartorial inspiration and suitable symbols of collective allegiances. Italian football fans now adopt some aspects of the dress of the British "hooligan". Badges on the denim jackets of Neapolitan "Ultras" declare the wearers as "Boys Fyghters", and traditional scarves are now much in evidence. The Punks, with their singularly elaborate, mutilated sense of elegance, are to be found in the clubs – if not the streets – of most major European cities. Even New York youth, seeking a sense of belonging in clubs such as CBGBs, now adopts aspects of the British Punk style for which, in fact, their predecessors provided the original inspiration.

Opposite
A Masai girl being decorated in the
traditional style of her tribe. The light V-
shaped markings on the face, together with
her beads and necklaces, make her
immediately identifiable as belonging to a
particular group.

The style of each youth tribe evolves in order to distinguish one group as
clearly as possible from another. The style of the Skinheads, for example, was a
direct reaction to the long hair and flared, embroidered clothing of the Hippies.
Skinheads shaved their heads and adapted the working clothes of the manual
labourer so as to maximize the difference between themselves and the middle-
class, radical drop-outs they so much despised. The Punks cut up their clothing
and painstakingly reassembled it with safety pins in order to distance themselves
from their clean, smart peers who had opted to stay in "the system".

This process of tribal differentiation is very much akin to speciation, which is
most evident among birds. Where a single species of birds inhabits, say, a small
island, its members tend to have a very dull plumage, lacking in pattern and
colour. As the number of species or subspecies in any one area increases, so too
does the number of species-specific markings in the feathers and beaks. The most
extravagant patterns and colours of plumage occur when the variety of avian life
in a given area is greatest and the need for identification becomes highly
important. Youth groups are, in this sense, very much like species of birds –
although, of course, their decoration is of cultural rather than genetic origin. The
need to develop a social identity is greatest around the time of adolescence,
especially within the "super-tribes" of modern nations. In order to increase the
distinctive character of a particular youth tribe, and the personal satisfaction
which comes through membership, tribal members adopt the equivalent of a
plumage that is in direct contrast to that of other contemporary subcultures.

As we get older and our social identities become more stable, our tribal
affiliations are usually signalled using less ostentatious clothing. Other channels
of communication are open to us, such as the way in which we decorate our

Below
The seemingly bizarre clay mask adornment
of the "frog men" from the Asaro Valley in
the Central Highlands of New Guinea.

Page 70
It is considered chic and stylish by some
people in modern societies to wear "ethnic"
jewellery and to include traditional tribal
artifacts in their "designer" apartments.
Here a Wopkaimain chief from the Star
Mountains turns the tables by wearing a
western designer pen in his pierced nostrils.

Page 71
An elaborate face-mask, worn for ritual
occasions by a Dei clansman in Papua New
Guinea.

houses, the cars we choose to drive and the objects with which we surround ourselves. Even so, the most taken-for-granted items of everyday clothing – the tweed skirts, green boots, cloth caps, corduroy trousers, blue collars, white collars, pinstripes and cardigans – all speak of our need to be a member of a group which has a human scale.

ADORNMENT AND DECORATION

The adornment and decoration of the human body features in all known cultures and societies: the practice is as old as recorded history. Figurines from Southeast European Neolithic cultures show elaborate spiral decorations on the face and head. The ancient Egyptians were skilled in the art of face-painting and make-up, using substances and colours which would not be out of place today. Ancient Britons dabbed woad on their faces and hair (predating the blue rinse by several millennia!). The Greeks and Romans similarly used whatever materials that were to hand in order to alter their physical appearance.

Some forms of adornment are used for the purposes of sexual attraction, particularly by women. Lipstick, for example, allows the mouth to mimic the genital labia, which are generally hidden from view for reasons of modesty. Application of colours to the area around the eyes, using shadow and mascara, draws attention to the emotional responses signalled by this part of the face. General facial make-up, while it can conceal blemishes, also creates the illusion of ruddy health. Men, of course, are not exempt from such adornment practices. Shaving and hair-styling are common among males throughout the world, even though they rarely have any practical function.

Bodily adornment is a universal channel of communication. Each culture develops its own "dialect" of this language, producing appearances which not only serve to enhance individual attractiveness but also indicate tribal roots. Features that are considered beautiful – and therefore enhanced through decoration – in one society are often seen as quite ugly in another, and therefore masked or left unadorned. Certain Mongolian races, for example, consider their own facial characteristics to be the height of beauty because they resemble those of the horse, which they regard as a masterpiece of creation. In other cultures, to say that someone has a face like a horse's would be deeply to insult them.

Not only is the face highly visible, its appearance is relatively easy to manipulate. For this reason it is, in most cultures, the area of the body which receives the greatest amount of decorative attention. Some traditional societies go further and alter the shape of the head, a process that is started at birth, when the skull bones are still soft. There is no consensus: some tribes flatten the head while others aim for an elongated or rounded shape. Such manipulation is almost exclusively carried out on the heads of female infants, the purpose being to make them more attractive in later life as potential brides.

The practice of head-shaping dates back thousands of years – it was present in pre-Neolithic cultures in Europe and Asia. It was a common feature of life for high-born women in ancient Egypt; Princess Nefertiti, for example, had a deliberately deformed head. Aristocratic Greek and Roman families often subjected their daughters to this painful and dangerous practice. In the latter case the aim was to accentuate those features of the head which were associated with high-class lineage and thereby increase the desirability of the young woman concerned. Head-shaping is still practised today in some societies in Africa, Greenland and Peru. Until relatively recently, it was practised also by

Opposite
A Nuba girl of Sudan, with the characteristic
beads and facial-skin disfigurements of her
tribe.

Opposite
Classic British Punk male and female, with characteristic "Mohican" hairstyle, studded jackets and other clear emblems of allegiance.

The dreadlocks of Rastafarians are central emblems of their culture and beliefs. The father provides his son with a strong stylistic role model.

various North American Indian tribes, who used boards and tapes to compress the forehead. It is thought that this process was the cause of a higher incidence of epilepsy and of blindness, resulting from the bulging of the eyes.

While head-shaping is one of the most extreme methods of altering an individual's appearance, other practices can effect similarly radical transformations. Discs of wood inserted into incisions in the lips of Botocudo girls in Brazil can create what is, to us, a totally bizarre spoon-bill appearance, with the distorted lips having a circumference of 60 cm (2 ft) or more. The men in some traditional tribes engage in equally disfiguring practices, although here the purpose is to emphasize their masculinity. Papuans, for example, use sharp sticks to bore holes through the septum of the nose so that they can wear decorative bones. Pierced ears, with holes sometimes broader than a finger, were until quite recently common among men of the Amazonian Cobeus tribe, who apparently used to store half-smoked cigarettes in them.

Decoration of the teeth is found among some aboriginal groups in Australia and New Guinea, and the male Ibans of Borneo engage in a form of dental manipulation which makes most Westerners wince even at the thought. The front teeth are blackened and then small holes are drilled from front to back, using a simple pointed file. Into these holes are inserted brass plugs, the ends of which are fashioned into star shapes. Finally, the teeth are filed down to sharp points. The distinctively transformed Iban man is now considered an object of beauty, and the pain he has undergone is regarded as but a small price to pay for such an enhanced appearance.

Some of these bodily disfigurements are, like circumcision, of special symbolic significance: they are part of the process of initiation into the adult world of the tribe. The more common styles of adornment, however, not only identify the role and status of an individual within a tribe but also announce that individual's tribal affiliations to outsiders. Where several tribes occupy a single geographic region, the styles become increasingly elaborate in order more effectively to differentiate between each of the groups. When a tribe has free range over a large area, and rarely encounters strangers from another clan, the need for such decorative identifiers is diminished.

HAIRSTYLES

In modern societies, decoration and adornment are most evident among young people, and especially among members of distinct subcultures. As each group vies with the rest to establish a sense of distinctiveness, the decorations become more and more intricate. While there are no recorded cases of deliberate modification to the shape of the skull in our modern tribes, most of the "primitive" decorative forms are used extensively.

Hairstyle is of special significance within Rastafarian cultures, for whom the dreadlocks are tribal identifiers. This cult was founded in Jamaica and embraces a belief in immortality: "We who are Rastafarians are the disciples who have walked from God from the time when the foundation of creation was laid, through 71 bodies to behold the 72nd house of power which shall reign forever." Also central to Rastafarian culture is the belief that the late Haile Selassie (Ras Tafari Makonnen, died 1975), Emperor of Ethiopia, is not only their spiritual leader but a deity in his own right. In addition, Rastafarians subscribe to the view that Black males are the reincarnation of ancient Israelites, now forced to live in exile because of "Whiteman". Jamaica is viewed as Babylon, while Ethiopia is seen as heaven. There is also a firm commitment to the idea of black supremacy and the inferiority of whites.

Facial decoration in Papua New Guinea. A Wigman applies yellow pigment in the traditional style.

The ostensible rationale for the deliberately unkempt appearance of the Rastafarians' hair comes from a passage in *Leviticus*: "They shall not make baldness upon their head, neither shall they shave off the corner of the beard, nor make any cuttings in the flesh." In the modern context, the hair of Rastafarians sets them apart from other people and signals the religious nature of their tribal bonds. It symbolizes their sense of being "natural men", unconcerned with modern notions of cleanliness and tidiness. More importantly, the dreadlocks represent rebellion and a refusal to accept the conventions of the dominant white population.

Even in its home culture of Jamaica, the Rastafarian style sets individuals apart from the majority. One anthropologist has suggested that, by wearing hair that is long and dishevelled, the Rastafarian is considered by others to be wild, dangerous, effeminate and dread-inspiring. The style reflects the essential contradictions of Jamaican culture and sets the Rastafarians apart from it. It also, of course, signals their membership of a distinctive alternative tribe, which has its own values and styles of behaviour.

Hair, in terms of both length and style, has been a consistent medium of tribal expression within British and European youth cultures since the 1950s. The wearing of long hair by males was particularly characteristic of the Beatnik and Hippy cultures of the 1960s and early 1970s. Long hair symbolized a rejection of "straight" culture and its values and provided the wearer with a relatively painless way of signalling his allegiance to an alternative culture. In terms of bodily decoration the individual was obliged to do very little except simply allow

Body painting in Brazil. A Xingh mother carefully creates distinctive zigzag patterns on her daughter.

his hair to grow long. Also, if need be, the hair could be rapidly cut off should the wearer wish to abandon the radical image – for example, to seek orthodox employment.

The reasons why long hair should be associated with protest and alternative youth cultures are fairly obscure. The impact of the doctrines of Christianity in Western cultures may, however, guide us to a partial explanation. Saint Paul, in his first epistle to the Corinthians, was instrumental in setting a stylistic trend which has continued, albeit with some notable exceptions, to the present day. While instructing his readers that women should wear hats during prayer, but men should not, he offered this justification:

> Judge in yourselves: is it comely that women pray unto God uncovered? Doth not even nature itself teach you, that, if a man have long hair, it is a shame unto him? But if a woman have long hair, it is a glory to her: for her hair is given her for a covering.

Saint Paul may very well have had a particular motive for this faintly ridiculous pronouncement. He was very keen to maintain strict gender roles within Christian culture, with women being relegated to a distinctly inferior position. For example, later in the same epistle he wrote:

> Let your women keep silence in the churches: for it is not permitted unto them to speak; but they are commanded to be under obedience, as also saith the law. And if they will learn anything, let them ask their husbands at home . . .

Hair-length was, therefore, a convenient way of reinforcing gender stereotypes and encouraging people to conform to the expectations of their sex.

For a man to grow his hair long has thus come to symbolize, in Western cultures, rejection of the concept of such narrowly defined masculinity, as well as a distaste for conformity. Hippies and Beats underscored the hair signal by

Few modern Punks achieve such a flamboyant display as this young man from the Rauepe tribe in Brazil. The plumage is attached to a mud cap.

Below
While this young man could easily regrow his hair and develop a more conventional style, the facial tattoos are almost impossible to remove. His adornment, which signals membership of a disaffected section of society, is permanent.

The elaborate headdresses and wigs of Kenyan Masai.

wearing clothes which similarly blurred gender differences. One effect of these signals was to attract the ridicule of the mainstream population, whose sense of solidarity was, in turn, reinforced by their distinction from the "long-haired weirdos". The Skinheads used the same medium, although the messages communicated were quite different, when they adopted severely cropped hair: this not only symbolized the "toughness" of their culture but also distinguished them quite dramatically from their Hippy contemporaries.

Shaved heads have traditionally been associated with disgrace and servitude: prisoners in many cultures around the world have been subjected to this practice not because it prevents the spread of lice but because it is a signal of their lowly position. Skinheads emerged as a British working-class tribe expressing alienation and disenchantment. The shaved head was, therefore, an ironic statement – a metaphor for their sense of injustice. In contrast to the "softness" of the Hippies, Skinheads announced their more determined opposition to authority and their readiness for violence. They also, of course, posed an embarrassing problem for school teachers. For years boys had been sent home because their hair was considered too long. Now boys were being excluded from class because their hair was too short! Authority figures were being made to look rather foolish, and clearly that was part of the exercise.

If head-shaving has traditionally been seen as demeaning for men, then women with shaven heads have been considered even more pitiful figures. For example, female collaborators in occupied France during World War II were

Make-up time in traditional style among Barzoana Indians in Colombia.

subjected to this humiliation as soon as the country was liberated. They were taken into the streets and publicly shamed, using in place of violence a process of disfigurement which was psychologically even more painful. Despite such considerations, however, female members of some youth tribes have voluntarily adopted the shaven head as a distinctive emblem of social identity. Skinhead girls emulated their male contemporaries to such an extent that virtually all gender differentiation disappeared (much as among the Hippies, although for diametrically opposite reasons). Some took pride in the fact that they had been refused entry to women's toilets because the attendant could not believe that they were female. Others added to this disregard for femininity by joining in fights and affecting a distinctly macho image.

Length of hair acts as a tribal identifier in this way only because of the traditions within Western Christian society. In many African countries it is the norm for women to have shaven heads, and at earlier periods of our own history the symbolic meaning of hair-length has been quite different. In virtually all cultures, however, hair has provided opportunities for both individual and collective expression. In the West we now observe extreme forms of hairstyling and decoration among young people of both sexes, many of which have explicit references to traditional, tribal styles. The "Mohican", for example, with its elaborate and coloured display, mimics a tribal symbol of a once mighty North American Indian culture. The use of gels to produce stiff spikes of hair has clear antecedents in the styles of Mali girls, and even the most dedicated member of the

post-Punk youth cultures would find it hard to emulate the elaborate styles adopted by the men of some of the traditional tribes.

TATTOOING

Like most forms of body adornment in modern cultures, hairstyling and -cutting involve essentially temporary changes to a person's appearance. However it has been manipulated, hair can be regrown in a matter of a few months. Make-up and facial paints are even shorter-term adornments: they can be removed with a cloth. Through the use of such adornments the individual can not only respond to changes in mainstream fashions but also quite easily change social affiliations. The long-haired radical can become a member of the "responsible", salaried majority simply by visiting the barber. The Skinhead can switch his allegiance to a new youth culture by letting his hair grow naturally. The Punk can apply for a job as an accountant as soon as he has removed his nose studs and tamed his hairstyle. A tattoo, however, makes a statement that cannot be silenced, and so in Western cultures tattooing is one of the most extreme declarations that can be made through adornment of the body.

Tattooing has a very long history. We know that it was used by the Thracians to indicate rank, and tattoo markings are evident on ancient Egyptian paintings and artifacts and on Japanese pottery dating back 3000 years. The practice is widespread in traditional cultures today and, although some forms appear to be purely decorative, most are commonly used as explicit tribal identifiers. Men in Samoa, for example, have no rights of status even after initiation until they have received their ritual tattoos. In some African tribes we find "insurance" tattoos

Tattooing in Japan was originally a form of punishment, the size and pattern of the indelible marking reflecting the gravity of the offence that had been committed. Today, *Irezumi* is an artform, involving depictions of peony and cherry blossoms, pine trees, landscapes, dragons, birds, tigers and other animals. Tattoos such as those displayed by the couple (*left*) and by the group of men (*opposite*) are rarely seen by outsiders. There is a saying in Japan: "The tattoo cannot guarantee happiness, must not be exposed, shown, burnt or erased. If this were to happen, the human body would die and its soul would err for ever without finding repose." For the men, the patterns are not only decorative but symbols of their allegiance to the underworld of the Yakuza.

on the foreheads of women: these are applied so that, if a woman is captured by a rival group, her origins will be clearly visible and she will be sold back to her own tribespeople. Similar marks worn by the men of such tribes serve exactly like military uniforms: they decrease the possibility of warriors being accidentally attacked by their own side.

In the Congo, children are tattooed soon after birth in a way which not only identifies them individually but also allows their tribal origins to be noted by others. This has very practical purposes; for example, children lost in the forest can be returned to their home village. In some cultures, however, only adults, and only those of higher rank and status, are allowed to wear tattoos. The more elevated the position of an individual, the more elaborate his decoration. Among the Maoris of New Zealand, elaborate facial tattoos were considered a mark of distinction and high esteem. In Melanesia, the number of lines in a facial tattoo is often related to specific achievements, in terms either of battle or of contributions to the wealth of the culture.

Conversely, tattoos have also been used to denote low caste or as a form of punishment. Up until the end of the 19th century it was common in the British Army for marks to be tattooed on soldiers who had broken military rules. The letters "BC" stood for "bad conduct", while deserters were indelibly marked with a "D". In many traditional societies, specific tattoos are also applied to the faces of men who have shown cowardice in battle or who have been caught stealing cattle from other members of their tribe.

While people in modern societies often subject themselves to tattooing for purely decorative purposes, tattoos, like other forms of adornment, can serve to indicate specific allegiances and loyalties. Being permanent embellishments, they also signal a high degree of commitment and loyalty. This is, perhaps, most strikingly the case among the Japanese Yakuza.

The Yakuza are essentially gangsters who live in the criminal twilight cultures of the major Japanese cities and, to a more limited extent, in migratory centres such as Hawaii and California. Their obscure name probably derives from a gambling term, "ya-ku-sa". In the card game *hanafuda*, "ya-ku-sa" means a particularly useless hand comprising a sequence of 8-9-3, making a total of 20, which always loses. At some point, "ya-ku-sa" came into general parlance to denote anything useless, and then it began to be applied to the gamblers themselves. The modern Yakuza, however, are a highly organized tribe whose scale of criminal activities is probably matched only by the Mafia. As well as conducting organized crime, however, they continue the traditions of the Samurai bandits through various ritual practices and, most visibly, through the wearing of extremely elaborate and colourful tattoos.

Tattooing in Japan has a long and respectable tradition. By the 17th century the practice had developed into a recognized art form, and intricate designs covering the entire body were popular among the Bakuto groups of professional gamblers. However, the original Yakuza tattoo was a form of punishment by the authorities, who aimed to identify criminals in such a way that they would be shunned by the rest of their society. In most cases, a black ring was tattooed on the upper arm for each offence which the individual had committed. The adoption of voluntary tattooing by the Yakuza was, therefore, an ironic reversal of the notion of the shameful symbolism of the enforced tattoo coupled with the maintenance of tribal traditions that derived from the Bakuto.

Tattoos covering most of the body are the ultimate tribal tie. Once the distinctive Yakuza style has been applied, the individual is forever identified with, and bound to, his chosen subculture. The association between gangsterism and these tattoos is so close that owners of public baths and saunas in Japan prohibit entrance to anyone who is tattooed. The Yakuza, however, have their own bathhouses, and for obvious reasons can be confident that few infiltrators will escape their notice.

The patterns of the Yakuza tattoos are famous for their fluid elegance, combining images of gods with those of heroes, animals and flowers. Depictions of celebrated Samurai warriors, in full battle regalia, feature strongly as reminders of the Yakuza's tribal ancestry. To produce such designs can take upwards of 100 hours of work with needles and inks, and the process is a painful one. This aspect of tattooing adds to the effect of achieving group solidarity; the endurance needed to withstand the pain and discomfort resembles that encountered in a traditional initiation ritual (see page 34). Once the individual has survived the ordeal, the tattoo takes on a doubly significant symbolic role.

By comparison with the practices of the Yakuza, tattooing in the Western world seems to lack style and intensity, yet it can serve substantially the same function. It is most commonly carried out among sailors and members of the armed services. Some of the emblems simply indicate attachment to a particular female, but many show allegiances to a particular regiment or service. Members of motorcycle gangs will often have the name of their chapter – the particular tribe to which they belong – engraved on their arm. Others choose symbols of virility or fearlessness: the combination of a skull and crossbones with the legend "Death or Glory" is a common example. The very act of tattooing itself also serves to denote a particular kind of individual – one belonging to a collective of people who engage in this minority style of adornment.

Members of contemporary youth cultures have been responsible for a revival of tattooing, but their reasons are a little different from those of their predecessors. Facial tattoos, in particular, are very visible statements which inevitably influence the ways in which others react to the person who is so adorned; for this reason, responsible tattooists refuse to work on faces.

Nevertheless, some of the more disenchanted Skinheads and Punks can be seen sporting spiders' webs, snakes and other "frightening" imagery on their cheeks and foreheads. The statement is clearly, if unconsciously, that the individual no longer cares about the future: he or she belongs to a special tribe which has not only dropped out but sees no possibility of ever dropping back in again. In this context, whether the facial tattoo is intended to shock or to beautify is irrelevant. Unlike the drop-outs of the 1960s, most of whom have now become members of bourgeois society, today's disaffected youth tribes are taking the business of permanent adornment to the same lengths as their peers in the traditional societies of Africa and New Guinea.

SYMBOLIC OBJECTS

While dress and adornment figure prominently in the ways in which we declare our tribal affiliations, we make use of a wide range of other symbols to reinforce patterns of collective bonding.

A "love hotel" in Tokyo, where the symbolic and expressive aspects of the car are rendered explicit. Here a Mercedes is provided as, quite literally, a vehicle for sexual fantasies.

Right
A consistent set of messages concerning lifestyle and allegiance is communicated simultaneously through different channels. The mode of dress, the Rolls Royce and the poodle seen here at Derby Day, England, instantly identify the owner of such emblems.

Opposite above
Many North American Indians aim to establish a balance of tradition and modernity, retaining important aspects of their culture while demanding a fairer share of the wealth and opportunities of North American society. This chief in traditional headdress stands next to a modern reminder of the wild horses that once roamed his native prairies.

Opposite below
The Bhagwan Shree Rajneesh, prior to his hurried and enforced departure from Oregon. It was the modest ambition of this charismatic religious leader to have a different Rolls Royce Silver Spur for every day of the month. Thanks to the generosity and loyalty of his tribal followers, a fleet of 85 such tokens of prestige was left behind to be sold off in lots.

Everyday functional items can become cult artifacts because of their design and their subsequent association with particular tribes of "cognoscenti". The Filofax, for example, is now a compulsory piece of equipment for people in certain groups and walks of life – especially when it is transported in an aluminium briefcase which contains also such cult items as a Rotring pen and a Braun calculator.

Deyan Sudjic has drawn attention in his book *Cult Objects* to the manner in which a variety of objects can be used as tribal identifiers, communicating a sense of affiliation among those who understand and share an appreciation of their inherent symbolism. He suggests that a cult object must, by necessity, be machine-made and mass-produced. Only in this way can its availability in sufficient numbers and in identical form be ensured.

Cult status is not necessarily dependent on the cost of the item, although some exclusive social tribes rely on the symbolism of conspicuous consumption to achieve a sense of solidarity. Sudjic points to the bottle of Perrier water and the packet of Gauloises cigarettes as typical cult objects. The Mark-2 Ford Cortina, a relatively downmarket car, is likewise seen as having served its purpose – uniting a distinctive section of British working-class society – a unity which excluded drivers of lesser cars, such as the Vauxhall Viva and the Austin 1100.

Nor is it the case that a cult object needs to show refined design or aesthetic form. Kitsch *objets d'art* achieve cult status primarily because they are the anathema of good taste. They constitute an ironic in-joke shared by those who feel that their sense of taste is so refined and secure that it can be the subject of self-parody.

Among the other items so discriminating that they act as clear emblems of allegiance are Leica cameras, Burberry raincoats, Marcel Breur chairs and Swiss Army penknives. One could easily add further examples of modern, and not so modern, esoterica. Many other artifacts can be used as indicators of allegiance among the modern tribes – the style in which one decorates one's home, for example, or one's possession of a coffee-making machine; because of its public visibility, the car is perhaps the most important indicator of all. From this point of view, we are what we own. When sufficient numbers of people all own and revere a single item or set of items, they create social tribes which have all the characteristics – bonds, alliances, shared customs and lifestyles – of their counterparts in traditional cultures.

On the surface, the automobile is simply a mechanical object which serves as a relatively inefficient mode of personal transport. In reality, however, it is one of the most powerfully symbolic objects to have been devised in modern cultures. It allows both men and women to make individual and personal statements about the kind of person they are – it is, quite genuinely, a vehicle for self-expression. However, the car serves also as a highly distinctive emblem of allegiance – a mobile and very visible indication of an individual's subscription to a particular group or class.

The car was originally a token of wealth, bestowing prestige on its owner and indicating his membership of a fiscal and social elite. In industrialized societies, as this means of personal transport became more freely available to the masses, largely as a result of the enterprising philosophy of Henry Ford, the car gradually acquired a more complex and sophisticated symbolic value. The choice of a particular model has become a part of the process of creating a social identity. We have increasingly become accustomed to judging people, in part, by

Despite their wealth, power and influence in the modern world, these ministers from the OPEC states dress and take meals in the traditional Arabic style.

the style or model of car which they drive – or even, in some cases, by their refusal to drive a car at all.

This process of automotive social identification is most apparent at the top end of the market, where certain luxury cars are clear talismans of style and sophistication. The modern British Yuppie, for example, must necessarily drive a Porsche in order to maintain proper appearances and signal his commitment to that distinctive tribe. To drive, say, a Jaguar or an Aston Martin would be to make an inappropriate statement, one which clashed with other tokens of Yuppiedom, even though either of the latter cars would certainly cost more than the Porsche.

Britons are familiar with the idea that the Rolls Royce denotes wealth and power. The drivers of such cars are clearly identifying themselves with a minority tribe and welcome the attention they get from other motorists and onlookers. There is, however, another signal conveyed by the Rolls Royce. The driver is a member of a rich elite, but his wealth is usually founded on "new money". Rather like the Cadillac driver, he is an *arriviste*, a man who has earned his money rather than simply inherited it. In class-divided British culture, a need therefore arises for those with "old money" to distinguish themselves from these new arrivals on the wealthy scene. The Bentley provides them with a very appropriate tribal identifier. It communicates the same sense of prestige as the Rolls Royce, but it does so in a quieter and less ostentatious fashion, better in keeping with the more modest rituals of the aristocracy.

In the United States, the automotive symbols of tribal allegiance are even more distinctive. Compare, say, the advertising-agency executive in his BMW or Mercedes with the gas-station owner, of equal wealth, in his Cadillac. Immediately we can tell which is which because the things that we associate with the owners of these cars are quite distinct. Cadillacs are for the brash *nouveaux riches* – the lower-class boys who have made good and who wish to declare their arrival in a new income bracket. The BMW likewise signals wealth and prestige, but in addition it communicates images of a more sophisticated lifestyle. The owner of such a car belongs to a quite different tribe, whose dominant values and attitudes are totally distinct from those prevalent among the Cadillac clans.

In this sense, we are what we drive, although many of us would want to deny it. Even the owners of rusty Volkswagen Beetles, Morris Minors or Citroen 2CVs make a clear statement of the kind of person they are and the automotive tribe to which they belong. Such cars fit with a particular chosen lifestyle, one in which the dominant image is that of being a caring, nonmaterialist person; ironically, perhaps, it is through the car that this anti-car statement is expressed most loudly. People who drive such vehicles are easily seen as belonging to a distinctive group; some further emphasize their solidarity by bonding together in clubs organized for the owners of such marques.

Even in the middle ranges of cars, we find subtle differences between the images associated with the various makes and models. A Fiat and a Ford may cost the same amount of money, but few would view the owners as being the same kind of people. Just as clothes speak loudly about our group allegiances, no

Even binoculars at race meetings have symbolic significance. In Britain, to be appropriate in such contexts the binoculars have to be large and of the "correct" make. Small binoculars, however sophisticated, can be the object of derision and scorn.

car keeps silent about the social characteristics of its owner. Cars may be things that we drive, but more importantly they are things that we *wear*.

An amusing way of demonstrating this particular symbolic function of cars is to ask people what they think would be the favourite meal of different car owners; for example, when BMW drivers go out to eat, what sort of restaurant do they choose, and what would they be most likely to order? In this way the unconscious stereotypes are easily revealed, as various researches have shown. Ford owners would probably opt for the traditional fare of roasts or chops. The 2CV driver is most likely to be a vegetarian, while Fiat and Citroen owners would tend to choose food of the same nationality as their cars. Cadillac drivers would surely order "surf and turf" – chunks of fillet steak with a lobster tail on top.

The thing about these stereotypes is that there is more than a grain of truth in them. This is because, when we select a car, we have in mind – albeit usually unconsciously – the group of people we would choose to join if we were given the option. If our perception of the typical driver of a given marque matches the idealized perception we have of ourselves, or the image we would *like* to have of ourselves, then we are likely to buy a car of that marque. By contrast, if the image created in our minds by a particular make of car is of a group of people with whom we would be uncomfortable, we bypass it and look at different models. Matters of price, economy, reliability and so on certainly play their parts in the choices we make, but in the end result it is our basic sense of group allegiance which dictates our choice.

DIET

The fact that we can associate particular tastes in food with ownership of certain cars clearly indicates that our chosen diet likewise has a quite deep symbolic value. This becomes most apparent when we examine the dietary requirements of the major religious groups, each of which has quite particular – and to outsiders sometimes bizarre – rules governing what can and cannot be eaten. In some cases, the prescription or proscription of certain foods makes good dietary sense. As the anthropologist Marvin Harris has noted, the Judaic proscription of pork makes sense in the Middle East: pigs cannot sweat, and are therefore ill adapted to the heat of this geographical area; moreover, porcine tapeworms, which present a serious hazard to life, are endemic in hot regions. There are similarly good reasons for the Hindu reverence of the cow: this animal provides more nourishment while alive in the form of milk products than its meat can after its death.

Apart from these practical aspects, however, rules governing the consumption of particular foods serve mainly to reinforce the collective identities of religious groups and to distinguish them from the followers of other doctrines. Actively to subscribe to a codified set of religious beliefs is essentially to align oneself with a tribe of people who share such beliefs. The tribe may be vast in numbers and spread throughout the world; however, there exist also discrete social groups which are centred around churches, temples and other regional institutions.

Food habits bond believers together, and they add a whole dimension of tribal unity. This is perhaps most clearly evident in the complex set of rules governing both the range of foods which can be consumed by orthodox Jews and the manner in which those foods may be prepared and mixed. The specific prescriptions stem from the Torah, which contains the books *Genesis*, *Exodus*, *Leviticus*, *Numbers* and *Deuteronomy*. The Torah is the most sacred of all books in

Judaism; the word "Torah" itself means guidance. Among these writings we find a clear distinction between "clean" and "unclean" animals – in other words, those which can be eaten and those which cannot.

In order for an animal to be "clean" it must both have cloven hooves and chew its cud. This effectively excludes pigs which, although they have cloven hooves, do not chew their cud; conversely, camels are excluded because, while they chew their cud, they do not have cloven hooves. Other excluded foods which are eaten and enjoyed by many non-Jews include birds of prey, most reptiles, winged insects and rodents. Fish, in order to be classed as edible, must have both fins and scales, which means that the eating of eels and shellfish is prohibited.

As well as restricting the individual's potential diet, the dogma of orthodox Judaism gives explicit instructions concerning both the slaughter of animals and basic culinary practices. Blood, for example, is considered sacred and its consumption is therefore taboo. This means that the blood of an animal must be completely drained during its slaughter, something done in ritual fashion by a Shocket, whose activities are supervised by a Rabbi. The throat of the animal is slashed and its body is left to drain. To be truly "Kosher", however, the blood which remains in the meat tissue must be removed by soaking, salting and final rinsing. Only then is it fit for cooking and eating.

The laws related to the cooking of meat mainly concern the need to keep it separate from dairy products. Not only is it forbidden to prepare a dish containing both milk and meat, it is necessary also to have two complete sets of utensils so that the two types of food can be prepared in total isolation. Furthermore, after eating meat an orthodox Jew must refrain from consuming any milk product for at least six hours; a post-prandial cup of white coffee or a dessert containing cream is therefore barred.

To an outsider, such practices may seem quite unnecessary for the maintenance of health and hygiene – indeed, even a little bizarre. Obscure references to lines in *Deuteronomy*, such as those warning people not to seethe a kid in its mother's milk, are quoted in justification of the Kosher rules, but non-believers find them unconvincing. This, however, is precisely the point of the elaborate rules and rituals. They are not there for health or functional reasons; rather, they are symbols of the collective unity of Jews. During 2000 years of relentless persecution, members of Jewish communities have retained their religious and social identity in many ways, one of which has been through adherence to well codified methods of food preparation.

Similar laws governing the range of food products which can be eaten and the manner in which they should be cooked are found in Islam. The rules governing slaughter are almost identical to those which direct the procedures carried out by the Jewish Shocket. The Koran forbids the eating of pork – indeed, the pig is such an abhorred animal that it is referred to as the "black one". However, there is a major dietary rule distinguishing Muslims from Jews: the proscription against drinking any liquid which contains alcohol. Instructions on *how* to eat likewise set the two religious groups apart: Muslims are instructed to eat only with their right hand and with their shoes removed, and to lick the plate at the end of the meal.

The best known Hindu eating taboo is rooted in reverence for the cow. The code of Manu which, among other things, prescribes various food practices, lists the slaying of cattle as an act of perversion; anyone guilty of it must undergo severe penances. The fact that this particular animal is singled out as being especially sacred probably has much to do with the utility of cattle in the agrarian culture of early India. The cow pulled the plough and provided milk; its dried dung was burned to heat homes during the winter. However, Hindu mythology contains a quite different explanation: the cow was created by the god Brahma on the same day as were the Brahmins, the highest of all castes in India, and so it has to be afforded the same status as the members of that caste.

The caste system is itself reflected in the dietary distinctions between Hindus of different statuses. Brahmins, occupying the most privileged and senior positions in Indian culture, are mostly vegetarians – to the extent that they even avoid eggs. Generally speaking, the lower one's caste, the fewer the prohibitions against eating meat (apart from beef, which is universally forbidden), although the system is complicated by further religious influences. The particular god worshipped by a family may dictate whether or not meat can be eaten and, if so, which animals are "clean". Pigs and chickens tend to be avoided by most Hindus in the higher castes, partly because of religious doctrines but also because of the scavenging nature of such animals. Other foods which are proscribed in all but the most lowly castes include mushrooms, onions, garlic and turnips.

The dietary habits of Hindus can be seen as direct indicators of rank and status within the complex caste hierarchy. As we have seen in the case of clothing and adornment, the individuals of highest status in traditional cultures are sometimes those with the simplest styles of dress and decoration. The vegetarianism of the Brahmins reinforces their position through its symbolism of their simple devoutness and their closeness to Brahma.

The caste system is further reinforced by traditions governing food exchange. Generally, a Hindu will not receive cooked food from a person of lower caste, although raw vegetables can be accepted. It is said that even the shadow of a low-caste person falling on the food of a Brahmin makes it unfit for consumption. There is an exception, however: ghee, or clarified butter. Because this comes from the cow it is sacred, and therefore cannot be defiled by the touch of even a member of the very lowest caste.

Christian groups tend to be more varied than those of the orthodox Jewish and Hindu religions, and this is reflected in the diversity of symbolic roles played by foods in Christian communities. Roman Catholics, for example, were until recently forbidden to eat meat on Fridays, although this rule has now been relaxed so that it covers only the period of Lent. Even so, a Friday offering of fish and chips is still the rule in many school and factory canteens, showing a continuing sensitivity to Catholic culinary habits.

FOOD CEREMONIES

Seventh-Day Adventists have perhaps the most formally coded of all Christian eating habits. Some of these resemble those of Jews. For example, the Sabbath is celebrated on a Saturday and, because it is a day of rest and contemplation, the main meal for that day has therefore to be prepared on the Friday.

The basic diet of most Seventh-Day Adventists is vegetarian, although eggs and milk products are permissible. This is in line with the belief in healthy living encouraged by Saint Paul. Beverages such as tea and coffee are generally avoided, along with spices, pepper, mustard and other condiments thought to be harmful to the digestive system.

In other strands of the Christian religion, meat-eating is not only common practice but is actively encouraged at times of ritual feasting. In most cases,

To many Papuans the Duke of Edinburgh has cult status, as exemplified by this reverent display of his photograph.

however, there are also prescribed periods of fasting during which many foods are specifically forbidden and a general degree of abstinence is demanded. The rules of fasting can be quite complex, as in the case of the Eastern Orthodox Church. Here, the normal 40-day period of Lent is preceded by a three-week-long pre-Lenten period. On the third Sunday of the pre-Lent period (Apkreos) and during the week following, each family consumes its remaining stocks of meat. On the following Sunday, all dairy products are finished off, and from now until Easter Sunday all animal products must be avoided. On two days of Lent – Palm Sunday and Annunciation Day – fish is allowed. Lentil soup is eaten on Good Friday as a symbolic reminder of the tears of the Virgin Mary; it is served with vinegar, representing the drink given to Christ on the Cross. When Lent finally ends, the celebrations begin with a soup called Mageritsa, made from offal, followed by a meal of roast lamb. Round loaves of bread are ritually decorated with boiled eggs which have been coloured red to symbolize blood.

Such food rituals are very reminiscent of those found in traditional cultures, and they serve the same symbolic function. For example, among the Samburu, who live in the rather arid regions of northern Kenya, there are clear rules governing what foods can be consumed during the initiation periods. The only meat which is allowed to novices is mutton. Unlike the normal eating style, which is with the fingers, initiates are required to eat the mutton using sticks.

In some traditional cultures, food can take on specific, magical properties in certain ritual ceremonies. For example, the vegetable curries served up to young initiates in various New Guinea cultures are intended not simply as sustenance but to protect them while they are in conditions of danger. Sometimes the eating of meals is specifically designed to emphasize status or gender roles within a tribe; for instance, among New Guinea's Wogeo islanders ceremonial roast meats are denied to women on the basis that the women would be poisoned by them.

The anthropologist Margaret Mead has commented on the symbolic function of food in marking the arrival of puberty among girls of the Manus of New Guinea. At the onset of menstruation, a girl is forbidden to eat certain puddings, such as tchutchu and those made from taro leaves; also, she is expected to abstain from a fruit called ung and from shellfish. Those meals permitted to her must be cooked on a separate fire in utensils specially set aside for the purpose. At the end of the first five days, a feast is prepared for the Manus girl; its aim is ritually to free her from her taboos. The meal – which consists largely of sago made into cakes – is consumed in a party atmosphere. Seven days later there is a second feast, consisting of three types of food. Taro and coconut-oil puddings are offered alongside cakes made from coconut and sago and from taro and coconut, all carefully laid out in carved wooden bowls. Finally, bowls of soup and fish are exchanged by those taking part in the ceremony.

The final marking of the transition from childhood to womanhood, which occurs after a further five days, again involves the preparation of taro, this time decorated with betel nuts. The girl is fed by her maternal grandmother, who chants and sings of the ritual role which the taro plays. Preparations then begin for the young woman's betrothal and marriage ceremonies, which likewise revolve around the exchange and consumption of progressively more elaborate foods.

The symbolic role of food in a modern society is most clearly shown in Japan – a society which, despite its modernity, still clings tightly to traditional rituals and ceremonies. Food is prepared and presented in what to Westerners can appear to be an obsessional regard for form and appearance. It is, however, in the traditional tea ceremonies that we find the pinnacle of social rituals.

To Westerners the form and rigid details of the Japanese tea ceremony are of a truly inscrutable nature: like Zen, the ritual simply cannot be accurately comprehended in the terms and concepts available to users of Western languages. There are no direct translations of many Japanese words and phrases; moreover, without a full understanding of the cultural context in which the tea ceremony takes place, the event must of necessity remain opaque and enigmatic.

Its purpose, however, is quite clear. Like all rituals, it serves to convey distinct messages to the participants. It is at one level a purely aesthetic and mystical experience, lacking in any apparent logic but constituting an art form in its own right. At another level, however, we can see the valuable role it plays in uniting people in the collective pursuit of not only a high level of consciousness but also group identity. To understand the way of tea is to belong to a highly distinctive collective which embraces the values of Zen teaching and which seeks a contrast with the ever-growing westernization of Japanese society.

There are several schools of tea in Japan, each with its own characteristic variants of the ritual. The differences are, in fact, quite small, but they are highly significant to the participants. In all cases, however, the ceremonies are so elaborated that people must be generally initiated into them through *okeiko* (formal lessons). In these the novice is introduced to each minute aspect of the ceremony, such as how to wipe a tea bowl, how to sit and, in the early stages, how to perform the relatively straightforward *usucha* (thin tea ceremony). At this "undergraduate" level, various diplomas and certificates are awarded as increasing degrees of skill are mastered. These in turn endow the recipients with finely graded levels of status and rank.

Students of tea get the opportunity to practise their skills at *chakai* tea gatherings, which offer various forms of the rituals to participants. In many cases a company or organization will book such a ceremony for its employees or members. Central to the purpose of these events is the notion of *tatemae* (social graces). The ceremonies focus on highly formalized patterns of interaction and etiquette which create social harmony and reaffirm collective bonds. The ritual serves as a channel for the expression of good intentions towards others and makes explicit the commitments of individuals to the group.

The full tea ceremony has an extremely complex structure and involves several stages, each of which has its own symbolic meaning. Dorinne Kondo of Harvard University, herself trained in the way of tea, has provided a detailed analysis of these components and identified the symbolic functions which they play.

In the Ura Senke school, for example, there are nine stages and the ritual lasts for several hours. The preliminary stage is known as *zenrei* and involves the issuing of invitations a week in advance of the ceremony. There is always a principal guest, who is expected to call on the host in person to acknowledge the invitation. On arrival at the tea garden, the guests wait until paving stones at the entrance are sprinkled with water before walking to a room in the outer garden to change their clothes. The group puts on clean socks and then moves to a waitingroom. Here the principal guest (*shokayaku*) leads the rest in single file as they walk towards the gate leading into the inner garden, which gate has been left open by the host. Once inside, the group advances to a stone basin to purify their hands and mouths with water.

The next stage, *seki-iri*, requires guests to take their positions. This involves entering the tea room through a low doorway; it is suggested that the necessary stooping is intended to express the guests' humility. This stage is followed by *shozumi* – the ritual arrangement by the host of the charcoal over which the water is to be heated. *Kaiseki* is the stage at which the guests are provided with food; each guest receives a tray on which are arranged a bowl of rice, soup, and dishes of vegetables and fish. The host does not join in the meal but stays to serve sake. The guests now move out of the tea room to wait once more in the garden; this point in the ceremony is known as *nakadachi*, or "middle standing". The sound of a gong signals the time to return to the tea room to engage in *koicha*, the peak of the ceremony. Here the thick tea is prepared, great attention being paid to the precise details of the ritual – for example, the correct purification of scoops and tools used. The guests drink in turn from the same bowl, which is wiped each time before being returned to the host. After the tea has been consumed, the fire is rebuilt; this is the stage known as *gozumi*, and immediately precedes the final stage, *usucha* (thin tea ritual). The principal guest calls on the host to end the ceremony and all the utensils used during it are taken out of the room in the exact reverse order to that in which they were brought in. Formal leave-taking is made with silent bows, and the host remains at the doorway until every guest is out of sight.

The complexity of such ceremonies has much in common with the religious rites practised in Western churches. However, although it is shrouded in Zen teaching and tradition, the tea ceremony is essentially a social occasion during which the bonds between the participants are strengthened through their collective knowledge of the ceremony and their engagement in the ritual.

In both traditional and modern societies, the sharing of food and ritual meals serve to perpetuate systems of myths and religious doctrines and to provide symbolic accompaniments to rites of passage – as witness the traditional foods served at a bar mitzvah. In modern societies, however, the role of food in providing collective unity is not restricted to such "sacred" contexts and events. In the secular world we can observe the powerful roles which meals and eating styles play in developing and maintaining tribal bonds.

This is clearly seen in dinner parties – those ritual events where food is the focus but where the reaffirmation of bonds and the satisfaction of social obligations are the true functions. It is virtually impossible in any modern society to invite a person to one's home without offering them food or drink of some kind. We invite people for coffee, tea, brunch or whatever – the unconscious rationale being that we thereby cover up the potential embarrassment of simply asking others to share a friendship. The dinner party is simply the most formal of such occasions. It may also have other functions, such as demonstrating status, wealth or even subservience: we invite the boss to dinner to show our recognition of his power and position, while at the same time, through the quality of the food and the presentability of our spouse, we hope to demonstrate our own status.

Shared eating does of course take on a distinctly ritualistic character among the modern Foodies tribes, whose social bonds are cemented by the sauces and sorbets of ever-changing tastes in *haute cuisine*. Among the Foodies a collective interest in gastronomic complexity and excess reaches cult status, a trend fostered in recent years by the increasing availability of "foreign" foods and movements such as *nouvelle cuisine*. For the members of the Foodie tribes – and

A celebratory Hindu feast in Madras.

the plethora of specialist cookery books bears witness to their ever-increasing numbers – a person is to be judged on what he or she eats. The abilities of translating a menu and selecting wisely from a wine list are the skills which act as tribal identifiers.

Comparing such modern tribes of gastronomes with the religious sects of traditional societies may seem a little far-fetched, yet the parallels are certainly there. The Foodies' bibles include the *Michelin* guides and the *Good Food* publications, both of which serve to identify the hallowed places in which the ritual foods are to be consumed. The serving of the food itself takes on the aura of a High Mass ceremony, while the *chefs de cuisine* make brief appearances in their role as high priests of culinary magic.

4 SEX AND COURTSHIP

A basic requirement of any human culture, whether it be "primitive" (in the sense that its development and sophistication are limited) or modern, is the regulation of sexual activity and relationships. Among other animals, the processes of mate-selection and reproduction are largely governed by instinctual forces. The females of most species are sexually receptive only at certain times, during which they give signals, in the form of scents, to announce to appropriate males the fact that they are sexually available. These signals "switch on" certain behaviours in the males. However, the process is a far from random one. In any sexually reproducing species there is the need to avoid the genetic pitfalls of sustained inbreeding; in other words, incest must be regulated if not obviated for a species to survive. Among animals this is achieved in various ways: genetically programmed responses, territorial distancing of offspring from their progenitors, the establishment of dominance hierarchies whereby access to receptive females is limited to males in the higher-rank positions, and so on.

Human societies achieve a similar level of regulation through rules which, although they may vary in detail from culture to culture, have substantially similar form and function. Such regulation is even more important in our case because, unlike the females of our nearest primate relatives, the human female is sexually receptive most of the time. It has been suggested that this rare trait arose as a by-product of our evolution towards a bipedal mode of locomotion. If we were to be able to stand on two legs, our bodies required greater secretions of hormones in order to stimulate sufficient levels of energy. In females, these same hormones are associated with sexuality and reproduction. As a result we have evolved as a species in which sexual activity is a more or less constantly available option.

This enhanced sexuality of the human race, some authors suggest, was itself partly responsible for the development of the tribal mode of living and of social interaction in general. The constant availability of sexually receptive females had the effect of increasing competition among men on a constant and sustained basis. This competition was an essential, adaptive process, but its regulation helped to tie both men and women more closely to their social groups. Group ties were strengthened by the governance of sexual activity by rules and taboos.

MARRIAGE

The universal human solution to the need to regulate sexual relations is, and for millennia has been, marriage. Marriage can be defined as a socially sanctioned sexual and economic union between two or more people. The transaction involves an explicit contract which provides rights of sexual access in return for the meeting of specific obligations. The human marriage contract is most usually between a man and one or more women. This being so, marriage can be seen not only as a means of regulating sexual and reproductive behaviour but also as a way of upholding male dominance. In the early hominid societies, it has been

An orthodox Jewish wedding. The tribal traditions of the culture are perpetuated in this modern restaurant, where the men are separated from the women by physical barriers.

suggested, males used mate selection and the establishment of a permanent bond as a way of exploiting the benefits of the foraging and gathering activities of females. Such a bond reduced the amount of labour which males needed to do, and thereby ensured the subservience of the females. Such attitudes toward gender roles are clearly evident in formal marriage ceremonies throughout the traditional and modern worlds. In addition, marriage is generally followed by child-rearing, which has normally meant the further isolation of women from the processes of power and authority in the mainstream culture.

As well as regulating sexual behaviour and, perhaps, keeping the balance – or imbalance – of power between the sexes fairly constant, marriages have a further function. Only rarely does a marriage relate to nothing more than the arbitrary union of two people: marriages involve also the establishment of alliances between two kinship groups. That this is true is clear from the ways in which we have developed linguistic terms to describe the relationships formed in this way. We use phrases such as "mother-in-law" and "brother-in-law", and through the very fact that we have such concepts we are able to understand the ways in which marriage serves not just to bond the husband and wife together but also to establish a clear set of expectations and obligations among members of the newly related families. This expansion of the network of relationships is central to the establishment of most tribal units. The Scottish clans, the power dynasties in the United States, the royal houses of Europe and the British aristocracy all depend for their survival on the careful development of appropriate alliances between

A Kenyan Samburu bridal couple holding the symbolic rod that symbolizes their new unity.

families which were originally founded on selective intermarriage and subsequent breeding.

Because marriage performs this vital function, spouse-selection is rarely left to pure chance or romantic whim. The characteristic Asian system is the formally arranged marriage. The concept of love is not central to the process of selecting a marriage partner, although it is expected that such emotional bonds will follow from the marriage union. We tend to think that in Western cultures the process is very different: people marry because they love each other, wish to stay together and want to raise a family. The reality, however, is very different. As in most tribal societies, we select marriage partners from a narrow band of people who share with us similar status, social class, values and lifestyle. There are exceptions – indeed, many exceptions – but the general pattern is remarkably similar to that which exists in societies where selection arrangements are formalized by the families of the couple to be married.

Arranged marriages are still very common in Japan, even within the affluent and Westernized sections of the population. In rural areas about 30 per cent of marriages consist of matches determined by the families of the two persons involved; these matches are known as *miai*. The big corporations, too, act as unofficial marriage brokers: many young women take low-paid jobs with little or no career prospects in large Japanese companies with the explicit aim of finding a suitable partner. The aim is not so much a romantic involvement as a secured economic future.

The main principles which govern who can marry whom are known as endogamy and exogamy. Put simply, endogamy means that people should marry within their own social group or category, while exogamy requires that partners should be selected from outside the immediate group. Traditional societies vary in the extent to which they practise one or other of these two types of marriage. Generally exogamy is preferred, but this statement should be qualified: whether a marriage should be considered as endogamous or exogamous depends on our definition of the boundaries of the group. Incest taboos and prohibitions, present in almost all cultures, prevent any significant degree of endogamy within the immediate kinship group. However, the rules vary when it comes to cousins and more distant family members. When we take a social stratum or caste as the basic group, then we find a pattern of endogamy in many cultures.

In Western societies there are well codified regulations which prevent endogamy within the nuclear family and its immediate extensions. But, if we look at rather larger groups, most of our marriages are endogamous. This tendency is not so strong as that found in the Indian caste system, where marriage between the castes is virtually unheard-of and women are generally denied as brides to other castes. Nevertheless, most Western marriages act to maintain stratum and class boundaries: the millionaire rarely marries the housemaid. Where marriages do cut across the boundary lines, we usually find that one or other of the partners is severed from his or her roots and incorporated into the other grouping. We see this most commonly when a woman marries a man whose family is of considerably higher status than her own.

Completely free choice of marital partners would rapidly break down a culture's social boundaries and so erode the delicate social fabric. Rigid endogamy, on the other hand, would lead to an intolerable level of inbreeding and threaten the development of the culture. Modern societies achieve a balance between endogamy and exogamy which is remarkably similar to that in the "primitive" societies. The basic forces which aided the evolution of tribal living are evident in modern societies, despite our illusions that we are free to marry anyone we love and that there are no constraints on our choice of sexual partners.

POLYGAMY

The other major distinction between types of marriage is that between monogamy and polygamy. In a society which favours monogamous relationships, marriage is a union between one man and one woman at any one time. Embedded in the religious rituals of marriage in Western societies is the notion that such unions are for life and that, once a mate has been selected, no other should be even considered. As we know, however, there are many cases where this ideal is not met. Apart from extramarital relationships, divorce and remarriage are common. For this reason, our system is usually referred to as serial monogamy: at any one time a person can have only one spouse, but the identity of the spouse may change from time to time.

In traditional societies, however, monogamy is a relatively rare arrangement. Polygamy is much more common and can take one of two major forms. The term "polygyny" refers to marriage between one man and two or more women. Such

Two traditional weddings. *Above*, the relative informality of a Palestinian marriage celebration. In contrast (*opposite*) is this highly formalized Japanese version, where the bride is treated as a princess for this one special day.

a practice implies that some men will necessarily never marry because of the relative shortage of potential brides. The number of wives an individual male will have will be directly dependent on his ability to maintain and support them. This system favours the older males, who may be able to support up to a dozen wives, at the expense of the younger men, whose social and economic status may effectively preclude marriage until their late thirties, if at all.

One problem arising from polygynous arrangements is the degree of hostility and jealousy between the wives. In some cultures this is overcome by establishing a separate household for each of the wives and their children. This is the case, for example, among the Tonga, where the husband's property and finances are equitably divided among the households. Among some Madagascar peoples, the rights of each of the wives are defined even further, with the husbands being required to divide their time equally among their wives. Those who break this rule, preferring to pass most of their time with a particular favourite, are deemed to be adulterous. In other cases, such as among the Lacandon of Mexico, order among the wives is established by a hierarchical system. The senior wives are afforded specific privileges, such as being allowed to carry flowers to the family shrines and having a degree of authority over the more recent additions to the marital home.

Strategies seeking to limit the problems of polygamous marriages are not, however, always completely successful. For example, recent research in Senegal by Daphne Topouzis has revealed the tensions which often exist in the households of Moslem families where polygyny is the norm. In some cases, where the husband can afford it, separate houses are provided for each of the

wives, but mostly wives share the same house and even the same bedroom. Topouzis reports that favouritism towards the newest or youngest wife is the cause of much strife. Sometimes older wives and their children are virtually abandoned by their husbands, retaining a status similar to that of a single parent.

Although polygamy in Africa arose in response to the social and economic needs of rural communities, the practice has been transferred virtually intact to the new cities, irrespective of the affluence of the men. Roughly one-third of Senegalese men have more than a single wife, and the system is seen, particularly by the males, as essential to the preservation of African traditions and culture.

Polygamy in the United States is, of course, illegal, but that has not prevented the most fiercely tribal of US religious groups, the Mormons, from establishing and continuing the practice.

The Mormons take their name from *The Book of Mormon*, the bible of the Church of Jesus Christ of Latter-day Saints, which was written down by the founder of the movement, Joseph Smith, in the 1830s. According to Mormon accounts, Smith was led by an angel to a collection of gold plates buried in a wood somewhere in New York State. These plates, covered in a strange set of hieroglyphics which only Smith could translate, described how a lost tribe of Israel had travelled to North America and were subsequently visited by Christ after his resurrection. Besides *The Book of Mormon*, Smith recorded a number of other divine revelations, among them the instruction that worthy Mormon males should take more than one wife, following the example set by the Old Testament prophets.

Pages 106–7
A Moonie mass wedding.

The Mormons' move towards polygamy took care of a couple of other social problems inherent in the movement and the times. More women than men joined the new religious movement and, due to the high rate of male infant mortality on the fringes of the North American frontier where the Mormons lived, there were significantly more women needing support. Even if we describe Joseph Smith's revelation as being just one more of the radical social experiments that were a part of mid-19th-century North American history or, more cynically, merely as a means to facilitate the satisfaction of male Mormon lust, we must recognize the behavioural change also as an adaptive response to shifts in the balance between the numbers of each sex. In the same way that basic structures in traditional tribal societies reflect, in a direct sense, the ecology and economic base of the culture, the religious dogma of the Mormons allowed the expansion of a modern tribe, which has indeed continued to flourish.

Joseph Smith was murdered by an anti-Mormon mob in 1844, and leadership of the church passed to Brigham Young. It was he who led his followers on the long trek across the Rocky Mountains to the inhospitable regions of the Utah salt deserts. Brigham Young is credited with having married 27 women during his lifetime (he died in 1877), although he was never married to this number all at the same time. It was under his direction, in the relative isolation of the western North American desert, that Mormon polygamy was at its most successful.

The practice of polygamy among the Mormons lasted, according to the official histories, for a mere 51 years. However, in Salt Lake City, the spiritual home of the Mormons, even today many men still defy the law and engage openly in polygamous marriages. Considerably more secretly continue the practice of plural marriage. The pressures towards conformity with the US norm, however, are strong and the official Mormon doctrine of "Living the Principle" was abolished in 1890 in order that Utah could be admitted as part of the Union. This was achieved by a further, and very timely, revelation to the president of the church cancelling the instruction concerning polygamy. Since that time, many polygamous families have been hounded out of Utah by fellow Mormons. These families have often fled to isolated areas of Montana, Arizona and Mexico, where closed, polygamous communities still flourish on the margins of US culture and operate as distinct, tribal units.

Polyandrous marriage, the other form of polygamy, involves one woman having two or more husbands and is encountered in only a few tribal societies, most of which are in southern Asia. In the blind valleys of the Himalayas, for example, this marriage system serves effectively to restrict populations which have nowhere to expand into. In some cases, brothers may share a wife in order to prevent dilution of family inheritance and wealth.

Although marriage patterns vary from culture to culture, the particular form adopted being primarily related to economic issues, they all serve to regulate and order sexual encounters. It is also the case, however, that in many cases the rules are broken, and there are few societies in which premarital and extramarital relationships are not found. In our own cultures, although in theory we subscribe to a monogamous system, we tolerate divorce, remarriage and extramarital affairs by both sexes, and we accept the reality of sex before wedlock. Our laws relating to inheritance now largely recognize the claims of illegitimate offspring, and bastardy is no longer such a stigma. However, despite all of these "modern" developments and areas of liberalization, marriage itself is still as central to our way of life as it is in the African village.

The author John Gillis compared modern marriages with those in pre-industrial Britain, and has observed that the usual assumptions about the gulf between them are quite unfounded. The view of 16th- and 17th-century marriages as pre-arranged and loveless matches turns out to be an over-exaggeration. Similarly, the notion of unconstrained courtship in the 20th century is also rather mythical. Parental control is still much in evidence when it comes to the acceptability of boyfriends and girlfriends, and the influence and direction of mothers and fathers are even more significant when it comes to spouse-selection. It is, in fact, during the 20th century that marriage has reached its peak as one of the most formalized rites of passage in our society.

THE WEDDING CEREMONY AND AFTER

The rise of overt promiscuity and cohabitation which originated in the 1960s and developed during the 1970s appeared to threaten the Western institution of marriage. However, all that really happened was that the preliminaries were modified. Marriage was often delayed, being preceded by a period of what used to be known as "living in sin". When couples did marry, the preference was increasingly for a large-scale ceremony with all its ritual and symbolism.

Traditional weddings have generally been the preserve of the more affluent members of modern societies. Lower down the socioeconomic scale, weddings have often taken the form of small rituals involving the exchanging of rings or other tokens, the gathering of friends and kin and witnesses, and even jumping over brooms. As an increasing proportion of the population now has sufficient financial resources, the large-scale wedding, in its formal, sacred and religious style, has become more widespread.

The form of the modern wedding, whether it be a lavish church affair or a more private ritual in a registry office, is much in line with that found in many traditional cultures, although the details vary. The wedding marks the culmination of a period of formal betrothal, marked by engagement and/or the calling of banns and announcements. There are exchanges of promises and vows, special clothes are worn, ritual foods are eaten and new relationships are created between the two sets of kinfolk. Reflecting the traditional idea of the dowry, the father of the bride is expected to pay for the entire ceremony.

The complexity of the marriage ceremony in traditional cultures varies considerably, as indeed it does in Western societies, but the overall pattern is generally easily recognizable and intelligible to outsiders. As the anthropologist Michael Howard has pointed out, such ceremonies can be as simple as carrying firewood to the door of a woman's family and subsequently moving one's hammock next to hers. The simplicity of such a ritual, which is practised by Tapirapé males, is, however, symbolic of the new understanding reached between the man and the woman and serves as an effective public announcement of their new relationship.

In more developed agricultural societies the ceremonies tend to be more elaborate, involving pre-nuptual rites, periods of seclusion of the bride, ritual foods and dress, and formal interactions between the two families involved. Also, there are likely to be processions through the streets, public announcements and ritualized, although generally private, forms of consummation of the marriage.

In modern societies, the marriage is most often consummated during the period known as the honeymoon. Instead of proceeding immediately to the new marital home, the couple isolate themselves from their families and friends. This is clearly to allow the rite of passage to be more firmly marked – in exactly the

A wedding party in Liberia. The influence of Western, Christian traditions is clearly evident.

same way that, in the case of initiation ceremonies, the young man is first separated from his tribe so that he may return with a new status and identity. The honeymoon similarly enables the newly-weds to return to their families and groups as people of quite different status and role. Their sexual involvement is now recognized – even demanded.

The anthropologist Robin Fox, however, suggests that the honeymoon might have an additional function. He points to the sense of ambivalence common in the relationship between the individuals who are being married and their future in-laws. The mother-in-law joke, he suggests, is universal and symbolizes the tensions which exist between wife-givers and wife-takers following marriages. The honeymoon, from this viewpoint, allows for consummation well away from the potential hostilities of newly gained in-laws.

In Japan, the relationship between bride and mother-in-law is particularly well defined, and is often a source of considerable distress to the newly married women. Nearly one-third of wives find themselves living with the husband's parents, mainly because of the shortage and high price of housing in urban areas. The daughter-in-law is expected to do most of the household chores and is subject to the complete authority of the husband's mother. She is often prevented from seeking a job, which effectively precludes the possibility of the couple being able to afford a home of their own.

The traditional form of Japanese weddings likewise illustrates the plight of women in that society. Although most marriages today are conducted in brief civil ceremonies, the traditional bride wore a white gown. In Japan white represents death and is the colour for funerals; the bride was therefore dressed in a manner which indicated the death of her past life. When she left her parental home, she was allowed to take only a mirror and her dolls, together with her carefully preserved umbilical cord (which would eventually be buried with her in order to secure her future in the afterlife). Stripped of her identity, she became the virtual slave of her mother-in-law.

One thing which symbolizes marriages in Western societies more clearly than anything else is the ritual cake. A recent study in Glasgow has shown that it is the single element which couples are least willing to dispense with, even when economic considerations might rule out most of the other trappings. The role of the wedding cake is equally significant in other cultures, and is central to marriage ceremonies in Cairo. Few people, however, have considered the real meaning of the traditional cake or investigated its symbolic role in any detail.

The form of the modern Western wedding cake dates back to Victorian Britain, and is modelled on the elaborately tiered structures consumed on other occasions by royalty and the aristocracy. Its neat order, with each tier diminishing in size towards the fourth (top) level, symbolized the values of our culture at that time. Each layer represented a distinct stratum of society, from royalty at the top to the masses at the bottom. In the context of the wedding ceremony it equally signals order, regularity and security – all those things so intrinsically bound up with marriage itself. The whiteness of the cake, like that of the bridal gown, is a symbol of purity.

What, though, are we to make of the ritual cutting of the cake? Some writers have suggested that cutting the cake represents the imminent loss of virginity which is (in theory at least) to be experienced by both partners. For this reason the bride and groom hold the knife together and, in joint effort, force it through the hard crust of icing into the soft, yielding layer of marzipan and then into the moist mixture beneath. As a metaphor for the sexual act it is far from precise, but there are sufficient similarities to make such an interpretation at least half-reasonable. The joint wielding of the knife could, however, be quite unrelated to the erotic aspects of married life, symbolizing instead the joint enterprise which is about to commence.

Whatever the true meaning of the cake – which, unlike that of the ring or rings used in the marriage ceremony, is not formally defined – its most important contribution is that it adds to the ritual character of the event. In modern societies we need opportunities for formal ceremonies, even though they may no longer be fashionable. Like our counterparts in traditional cultures, we need to celebrate the newly legitimized sexual liaisons between our friends and relations.

The role of marriage shows no signs of weakening in our modern cultures, nor do the principles of mate selection seem to vary much over time. The universal need for regulating sexual behaviour and for cementing the ties between families is met in substantially the same ways in all societies, whether traditional or modern. Our reliance on essentially tribal marriage practices continues to be revealed not only in the pomp of cathedrals and churches but even in the characterless anterooms of registry offices and judges' front parlours.

5 SPORT AND SPECTACLE

Sport in modern society is the child of the traditions of our hunting ancestors. Within stadia and arenas around the world we find both symbolic reminders of our origins and reflections of the cultural forces which have shaped so much of our development as social animals. Modern technology and the interests of large commercial institutions have come to dominate the organization and management of sports in most countries, but the true functions of sport are still manifestly evident in the nature of the games and in the ceremonies and spectacles which surround them.

Most sports involve skills which were once essential for survival within hunting communities. Speed and agility, coupled with an accurate aim and fine coordination, are characteristic of virtually all of the mass-appeal games. Additional requirements in many sports are territorial defence, stamina and physical strength. These skills and attributes no longer have much real function in a modern culture which relies so heavily on intellectual and technical abilities. Even so, we show no signs of abandoning the celebration of them. We preserve them in tribal rituals which deify the most skilled exponents and which bind groups together in collective support of their champions.

Sports can engender an extraordinary intensity of emotion among spectators. Utter despair is written large on the face of this French rugby fan.

SPORT AS RITUAL

Sports spectacles are central features of all modern societies. The anthropologist Alyce Cheska has drawn attention to the ways in which these modern rituals embrace the same components as those found in tribal cultures. These are, principally, repetition, regularity, emotionality, drama and symbolism.

The need for repetitive ritual is most apparent in traditional agricultural societies. Planting and harvesting are recurring times of considerable economic importance, and are therefore marked with distinctive ceremonies. Some of these rituals, such as those marking the yearly cycle, remain with us. Harvest festivals and spring rites still survive, although the spread of relatively modern religions has meant that they have had to adopt different guises. However, these celebrations are no longer such a central feature of our cultures. In a technologically sophisticated society the passage of time is measured in a different way. Sporting occasions, on the other hand, bring back a way of segmenting the year through the introduction of what are known technically as calendrical divisions.

In Britain, major divisions of the calendar occur with the onset of the football season in late August and its climax at the Football Association Cup Final in May. Because of the influence of commercial interests, this season overlaps with the traditional times for playing cricket, causing some dilution of the accuracy with which the seasonal changes are marked. In the United States, the sporting seasons are more directly related to the primeval system of dividing up the year. The football Bowls are held around the winter solstice, baseball finals occur around the autumnal equinox, and the basketball championships mark the onset of spring.

Regularity in sports is ensured through the rigid and invariant rule structure imposed upon them. Small modifications might be allowed, as in the case of changes in the rules concerning tackling and substitutions in soccer, but the format remains virtually constant. Major changes are strongly resisted by both players and spectators, who wish to preserve the security which the ritual activity provides. As in the case of other ceremonies, such as marriages, funerals and baptisms, there is a need to preserve continuity of experience – to establish the degree of routine predictability which is ever-present in tribal communities but which is often lost in the chaos of modern societies.

The rulebooks of sports are very much like religious bibles. They contain not only the "commandments" but also the basic tenets of sacred dogma and values. In soccer, for example, the rules determine the dimensions and shape of the "sacred" territory of the playing field and prescribe specific activities. While other clearly defined actions, such as handling the ball, are prohibited, there are more general prescriptions which determine the ethos of the ritual. The offence of "ungentlemanly behaviour" covers a wide range of possible acts which are in breach of the concepts of fairness and dignity that lie at the heart of the game.

Cheska comments: "A sport event probably represents the most remarkable display of fair play known today. The reason for this insistence on morality may be that sports are idealized make-believe versions of the real world." The interesting aspect here is the notion of idealization. We are unconsciously aware of what is missing from our cultures and seek to redress the balance – returning to the ideal through the rituals of sporting events and their echoes of our tribal past. The team we support represents an ideal community of people to which we can feel a sense of commitment and belonging.

The ritual channelling of aggression and the cooperative bonds between the players are evident in this rugby match between the British and New Zealand teams.

The seeming tranquility of bowls, seen here played in the south of England, belies the game's nature and its echoes of our hunting ancestry.

Emotionality is a most apparent and ever-present feature of sport spectacles. The drama of the occasions is highly charged with passion – both the ecstasy which comes from victory and the abject misery associated with defeat. In all but a very few sports (e.g., climbing) there is a winner, either an individual or a team. For those directly involved in the enactment of the drama there are special rewards and costs, but the same goes for the thousands or, through television, millions of spectators who share in the emotional experience.

Sporting events provide one of the few occasions on which ordinary people have the opportunity to engage in emotional risk. Lives in modern cultures tend to be ordered and regulated by impersonal processes and mechanisms. Deliberately sought-after emotional risk therefore brings, in the context of communal, ritual activity, a heightening of bonds between people and a sense of collective involvement.

AMERICAN FOOTBALL AS A RITE

The particular rituals and rites of collegiate American football have been thoroughly investigated by the anthropologist Shirley Fiske. She sees the sport as providing for those involved in the game a masculine rite of passage which is strikingly similar to those discussed in Chapter 4. Such rites take place within a yearly ceremonial cycle, with distinctive rituals to mark the transition from one status to another.

The American football cycle begins in September with what are termed "Double Days", because novices are required to practise twice daily; they are also isolated from females and restricted to a special diet in which certain foods

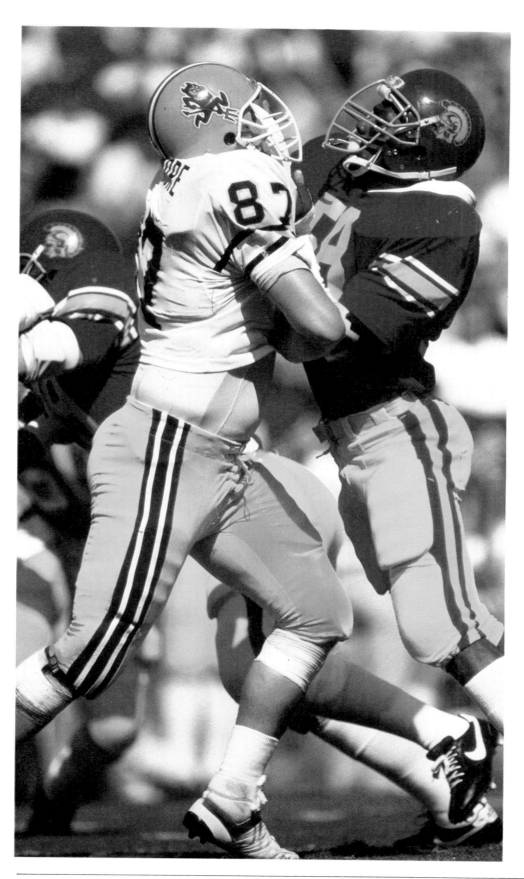

Man-to-man combat in American Football.

(such as potatoes) are taboo. Fiske presents the daily schedule in the way an anthropologist might describe the fixed rituals of an African tribal society. She notes how the novices meet in a "magical" location (the football stadium) dressed in special tribal costumes. The role of the elders (coaches) is to subject the young men to ritual humiliation and psychological harassment. This first stage in the transition process is akin to the symbolic "killing" in traditional initiation ceremonies where the novice is "dead" to the rest of his tribe.

The season itself involves weekly confrontations with novices of similar age from rival tribes (teams). Such conflicts are ritualized and constrained by well understood rules. Even though the novices continue to mix freely with other members of their society, their behaviour remains constrained by taboos concerning food and contact with women immediately prior to the ritual battles.

Physical punishments are inflicted on the young men during the ordeal of training, which takes place at regular, prescribed intervals. They are, however, allowed to avoid some of the normal duties in the "frats" (fraternity houses) in which they live because of their special transitional status. Their achievements on the playing field, which result in the ceremonial adulation of the initiates' peers, also offset some of the pain and deprivation involved in the rite of passage.

Towards the end of the season, preparations are made for the final ceremonies. Group seclusion is intensified, although members of the most successful sides are now given suitably prestigious accommodation prior to the "glory" ritual of the Bowl game.

Following the final ceremonies, there begins a "latency" period during which the novices are released from the strictures of isolation and ordeal. They are, however, still closely monitored by their coaches, who look for signs of maturity and a sense of manly responsibility. The final stage of the transition rite arrives with the advent of what is known as the Spring Ball. Here the novice has the opportunity to compete as an *individual* for his place in the team for the coming season. During this stage he is no longer subject to seclusion or taboos, but his future status in the football tribe will be determined. Moreover, this final stage allows for a process of reintegration, in which the novice gradually returns to mainstream society, having shown his willingness to subscribe to the propaganda and restrictions of his elders and having demonstrated his ability to endure the physical rigours like a man. He returns, in effect, as a new person.

SOCCER AND TRIBAL BEHAVIOUR
The tribal nature of American football is as much apparent on the field of play as it is behind the scenes and in the locker room. The game itself requires close cooperation, and bonds are reinforced through the learning of special plays, communicated in a code which is meaningless to outsiders. The essential skills are those of physical strength (when blocking or tackling rival players), accuracy of aim (when throwing passes or kicking field goals), and speed (when running with or intercepting the ball). As in the hunting clan, however, individual skills and attributes are of little value unless coordinated with the actions of others. In sport, as in hunting, team work, which relies on strong bonds forged between the participants, is essential for survival.

Similar reflections of tribal processes are found in European sporting contexts. The British football world, for example, has been analysed in depth by Desmond Morris in his book *The Soccer Tribe*. He suggests that it is a mistake to see the game of football as symbolizing a battle between two rival armies: in reality the two

Cheerleaders at an American Football game. In some cases their supportive role has a distinctly erotic aspect, presumably intended to provide additional motivation for the male participants.

groups are not trying to "destroy" each other but are, rather, attempting to get past their opponents in order to make a symbolic kill by shooting a ball into the goal.

Morris traces the roots of sports such as soccer to the activities of our primeval ancestors, the "survival hunters", who relied on the chase and killing to stay alive. When hunting for food became no longer necessary for survival, men became "sports hunters", keeping alive the thrill of the chase for its own sake. The third stage of development was marked by the "arena blood-sportsmen", who brought the hunting activities of the countryside into the centre of the cities. These were finally replaced in relatively recent times by the "arena ball-sportsmen", who adapted the rules and rituals of bloodsports to create more socially acceptable games.

Around the world, the earlier stages of the development of modern football are still evident. Hunting for survival is a way of life within a number of traditional societies. Sports hunting continues with the ritual chasing and killing of foxes and deer. The matadors of Spain and Mexico enact the macho rituals of killing bulls before appreciative urban audiences. Games like football, however, represent the ultimate ritualization of tribal hunting, removing death altogether but retaining the use of all the cooperative skills which once ensured our survival as a species.

The modern game of soccer has its more recent roots firmly in the folk games of medieval Britain and Florence. One of the earliest references to the English game

comes in a manuscript from 1175 called *Descriptio Noblissimae Civitatis Londinae*, written by a monk called William FitzStephen. Here he reports on the tribal contests between the apprentices and students, which had few formally defined rules and were more like opportunities to settle old scores and reaffirm patterns of group solidarity.

> All the youth of the city go to a flat patch of ground just outside the city for the famous game of ball. The students of every faculty have their own ball, and those who are engaged in the various trades of the city also have their own ball. The older men – the fathers and men of substance – come on horseback to watch the competitions of the younger men. In their own way the older men participate in the sporting activities of their juniors. They appear to get excited at witnessing such vigorous exercise and by taking part in the pleasures of unrestrained youth.

Football became more widespread in England in the 14th and 15th centuries, and its bloody, tribal nature attracted the increasing wrath of the authorities. Involving limitless numbers of rival players, the presence of a ball was almost incidental to the ritual. On Shrove Tuesdays and other religious festivals, lads from rival villages would engage in traditional battles for dominance and honour. The sport was condemned by sheriffs and religious leaders alike as a dangerous ceremony, but its function of channelling hostilities within a ritual framework was evidently recognized. In *The Anatomy of Abuses*, the Puritan Phillip Stubbs summed up the dominant attitude toward folk football:

> I protest unto you that it may rather be called a frendly kind of fyghte than a play or recreation – a bloody and murthering practice than a felowly sport or pastime. For dooth not everyone lye in waight for his adversarie, seeking to overthrowe him and picke him on his nose, though it be uppon hard stones? In ditch or dale, in valley or hil, or what place soever it be hee careth not so he have him down. And he that can serve the most in this fashion, he is counted the only felow, and who but he?

While Stubbs denounced the game, he clearly recognized its true function. It allowed individuals to gain reputation and prestige through the display of manly strength and "virtue". Although the sport was essentially a scrap between two sets of rival youths, it was also a "frendly fyghte", structured by traditional rules and understandings. Above all, it was closely linked to the rituals of religious festivities, blending sacred and secular aspects of life to express both tribal loyalties and fervent hostility towards rival clans.

RITUALIZED BLOODSPORTS

In contrast to team sports, spectacles such as cockfighting may at first seem an unlikely focus for tribal bonding. On the surface, the spectacle appears to be just a matter of two birds tearing each other to pieces in a pit watched by men who are seeking financial gain through the placing of judicious bets. In Bali, however, the cockfight has much deeper social and cultural significance, and this is reflected in the obsessional interest and passions which the "sport" arouses. Here the "kill" serves to focus complex patterns of affiliations, while the cocks themselves are central to the development of masculine status among Balinese men. The anthropologist Clifford Geertz has observed that, in the same way that much of US culture surfaces at the ball game, Balinese culture is revealed at the cockfights. This is because, although it is the cocks which are in physical combat, it is really men themselves who are fighting.

In the English language the word "cock" is often used to mean the penis. Among the Balinese the connection extends beyond linguistics. The cock (*sabung*) symbolizes manhood, and the word is not only used as a metaphor for the male genitalia but also has meanings such as "tough guy", "hero", "warrior" and "ladykiller". Most Balinese men spend many hours a day grooming and stroking their fighting bird, holding it between their thighs and occasionally exciting it by pushing it out towards another man's bird. Occasionally, one man will play with the bird of another; however, instead of the bird being passed to him, he will sit behind the other person, reaching around him to pet the bird as it sits between his legs.

The status of the cock is not simply that of an animal. In Bali culture, there is a distinct aversion to animals and animal-like behaviour. Even babies are prevented from crawling on all fours because of the association with the locomotion of animals. The cock, therefore, not only symbolizes the masculinity and ego of its owner but also encapsulates the ambivalent fascination with animality and what Geertz sums up as the "Powers of Darkness". The cockfight is essentially a blood sacrifice to appease the demons.

Whatever the symbolic functions of cocks and cockfights, the social functions of the "sport" are revealed in the complex patterns of betting which surround the fights. The owners of the two cocks involved in a fight place "centre" bets which most usually involve large sums of money. An owner may borrow from his kinfolk or members of his village in order to place the bet, but he must never make a stake unless he has the resources to pay in full should he lose.

Bets are placed by the spectators, too, and here some subtle cultural rules apply. A man should never bet against a cock owned by a member of his own kingroup; indeed, he will usually be obliged to bet in favour of it, even though any objective evaluation might indicate that it is likely to lose. The closer the kin ties, the greater the expected wager.

In cases where neither of the owners is from a person's kingroup, bets will be placed in favour of the cock owned by the person who belongs to the most closely allied group. This is extended to supporting any owner from one's own village in preference to an owner from another village. In order that the pattern of bonds can be systematically reinforced by the spectacle of the cockfight, there are few occasions when two "outsider" cocks fight each other. Similarly, there are seldom fights between two birds both owned by members of the same group.

Long-running feuds between rival groups are frequently expressed in open hostility at the fights and in the placing of excessively large bets. This form of ritualized conflict involves direct symbolic attacks on a rival's masculinity, as epitomized by the cock, and therefore on his social status. This applies particularly to the centre bets placed by the owners and their financial backers. If a bet cannot be raised among allies then it will not be made at all, because to be indebted to outsiders runs counter to the principles of betting, and the consequent affirmation of allegiances, central to the cockfights.

On the rare occasions when the two birds are viewed as irrelevant, because they are both owned by members of non-allied groups, betting still takes place. Some problems arise, however, since there is no clear guidance concerning which cock should be favoured. There is also the risk of betting in the opposite direction to one's kinsman. To avoid any embarrassment and potential social rifts, the tacit social rules prohibit any discussion between kinsmen as to how they have placed their bets.

An excellent example of the sense of trust that male bonding generates. Here a young man at the Pamplona Festival leaps from a tower into the safe arms of his peers.

The ritual framework which surrounds the cockfights combines surrogate duels between rival males with the "kill" of the hunt. A seemingly savage, cruel and pointless spectator sport turns out to be pivotal in the regulation of tribal bonds and loyalties among Balinese men. The contests between males are of such a highly ritualized nature that the possibility of injury is extremely remote – although spectators can sometimes become so engrossed in the activity of the cocks that they are caught a glancing blow by the razor-sharp talons affixed to the birds' legs. Such injuries, however, are quite rare, and are certainly not an intended feature of the spectacle.

In bullfighting, by contrast, the risks are far more serious. Men as well as animals face possible death, although the odds are stacked firmly against the bulls. The corrida most closely follows the hunting model in that a group of men is forced into a pattern of cooperative actions in order not only to ensure the killing of the prey but also to lessen the risks of losing their own lives.

Like other sports which illustrate the survival of male bonding, the bullfighting ritual has deeper meaning and significance to both the participants and the spectators. In Spain and Latin America the sport serves to reinforce central tribal values and to continue the dominant concept of machismo. The matador symbolizes the warrior/hunter in his fearless acceptance of challenge and danger and in the skilful manner in which his courage is demonstrated. It is not simply physical strength which is celebrated in the corrida – many famous matadors have, in fact, been relatively puny individuals. What inspires the crowds who

The Pamplona Festival in Spain is an occasion for ordinary young men to exhibit their daring and skill as they challenge the bulls that run through the streets.

come to view the spectacle is the matadors' ability to use their wits and prowess with the sword in order to ritually slay the bull.

The contest between the matador and the bull also symbolizes something further: the resolution of conflicts between young men and their fathers. It is no accident that many matadors include in their "stage names" the nickname for child – nino – or use diminutive forms such as "Chico". The sociologists Louis Zurcher and Arnold Meadow have suggested that in Mexico the bull, with all its power and blatant masculinity, stands as a symbol of the father-figure, against whom the relatively much weaker matador, or son, competes for dominance and independence. The young male spectator at the bullfight can work through his anxieties over his masculine role and the fear he experiences concerning his father's domination. He can identify with the courage of the matador and, especially when the contest goes badly, he can also project onto the matador the accusations of cowardice which he himself has received from his father.

If the bull symbolizes the father and the matador the son in Mexican society, the audience can be seen as the mother figure. The matador, in dominating the bull, looks for approval to the spectators in the way that a son seeks his mother's reassurance when competing with his father. The drama of the bullfight is a re-enactment of the domestic struggles which characterize Mexican culture. The mother encourages the conflicts between father and son in order to promote her own sense of control. The audience at the corrida demands that the matador and bull fight to the death, and females have an opportunity to act out their aggression towards the males who dominate so much of their everyday lives.

From this viewpoint, the bullfight, like traditional tribal rituals, allows central features of culture to be passed on from one generation to another and to be fully understood and reinforced. This is particularly important in the Mexican example because of the pressures of modern influences which threaten to erode the cultural values and lifestyles of what has been traditionally a feudal and caste-divided culture.

The idea that it is the cultural messages conveyed by the bullfight, rather than the actual witnessing of ritual killing, which is important is illustrated by what some people see as the progressive emasculation of the spectacle. Ernest Hemingway noted that, as the corrida has developed (or decayed), emphasis has shifted away from pure killing to the subtleties of cape-work and the placing of the banderillas (the barbed sticks used to enrage the bull and force it to fight). The horses, which were once quite regularly gored to death by the bulls, now wear protective padding, and safety fences and rails are much more in evidence in the stadia. The point is now much more to dominate the bull and to tame its powers, rather than merely to slaughter it.

In Spain the bullfight has a similarly expressive function, although the details of the symbolism may be slightly different. As in Mexico, the Spanish bullfight has the function of reflecting and keeping alive key features of culture. The anthropologist Garry Marvin has noted that a central element of Mediterranean culture is the concept of honour, achieved through self-reliance. A man whose honour is affronted must immediately respond, using only his own resources to resolve the issue. He does not seek to involve the institutions of the state, for this would be to appeal to a "foreign" set of forces and values inappropriate for the management of social identities. Respect is won and defended only within the patterns of interaction between the individual and his peers.

This essentially tribal way of life, which persists even within the formal structures of the Spanish state, is given expression in the Andalusian and Catalan corridas. The action which takes place in the arenas symbolizes the ideal behaviour of men struggling to maintain honour in the face of challenge and difficulty. As in the Mexican case, masculinity must be demonstrated at all times. And, while the Spanish bull might not be so clearly perceived as a father figure, it still represents a powerful male – one which is wilful and difficult to control. As Marvin writes, "If the matador is able to meet the challenge successfully, he gains prestige and status, and vindicates his claim to be a true man. Failure brings insult, ridicule and a loss of reputation."

An interesting feature of both Spanish and Latin-American bullfights is the non-athletic character of the principals – the matadors. There is no cult of physical fitness or prowess, and training by matadors is generally frowned upon. Too much physical agility, it is thought, can spoil the spectacle. Machismo is not expressed through the ability to attack others. The matador is a man who *responds* to the charges and the naked aggression of the bull. In this way, he represents the ordinary man, who is able to withstand the pressures of male rivalry and maintain his all-essential dignity and masculine honour.

THE PALIO

The role of sports spectacles in uniting and defining tribal loyalties is extremely apparent in the flamboyant horse races held twice yearly in the Tuscan town of Siena. The Palio is central to the life of all Sienese people, whose history is steeped in the distinctive tribalism of the medieval city states which have now been absorbed into Italian culture. For hundreds of years, constant wars were fought between the armies of Siena and Florence, and lesser cities, such as San Gimignano, Montalcino and Montepulciano often provided the battle grounds for these encounters.

Stability came to Siena after the city's final defeat by the Florentine forces, although the Sienese still celebrate their earlier victories in this long-running struggle. In the 13th century, nine men were selected to rule the city and were instrumental in the economic and cultural development which followed. A central square, the *campo*, was built, and today this provides the circuit for the Palio. The *campo* takes the form of a shell with nine spokes radiating from its middle to represent the "Nine Good Men". At the rim of the *campo* stand the major buildings, including the cathedral, and narrow alleyways lead into the small streets beyond.

The city as a whole is divided into 17 districts, or *contrade*, whose populations even today are fiercely independent, tribal groupings, each the sworn enemy of the others. Ten of the *contrade* enter horses and jockeys in the race, and these career three times around the *campo* in just over a minute. The prize is simply a silk banner called the *palio*.

Described as baldly as this, it is hard to see the attraction of the brief spectacle. Yet the Palio is the very essence of Siena and its culture. The race itself is merely the culmination of year-long preparations and anticipation. The members of each *contrada* jealously guard their horses, for "nobbling" is a common occurrence. In the days leading up to the race, elaborate precautions are taken to prevent the horses being fed drugged food, and members of a rival group who are seen in the vicinity of the stable are likely to be seriously beaten.

Three days of feasting at tables set out in the narrow streets bring together every family within each of the districts in a show of solidarity and merriment.

A traditional Contrada flag being displayed at the Palio in Siena.

Some of the rows of tables stretch 400 m (a quarter of a mile), and there are no class or rank distinctions. Members of the local nobility sit jammed up against shopkeepers and tradesmen. Only the jockeys, the symbolic champions of the *contrade*, have special places, where they are fêted in the company of the most attractive females.

Prior to the race, each *contrada* parades through the centre of the town, ritually displaying tribal bonds and expressing open hostility to the other groups. Fist fights frequently occur between the rival sections. The horses are taken into the local churches to be blessed by a priest in front of the altar. To outsiders, a horse in the sacred confines of a local chapel may seem a bizarre, almost blasphemous, spectacle, yet to the Sienese it is central to the rituals of the Palio. When a horse decides to urinate or defecate on the marble floor, this is taken as a sign of good luck. Meanwhile, as the preparations near their climax, the bell in the tower of the Palazzo Publico is rung constantly in a manner which has been described as symbolizing the city's heartbeat.

Finally, the horses and their riders are assembled and race around probably the most dangerous course in the world. The horses frequently lose their footing on the slippery cobbles, and jockeys have been thrown into the barriers and killed. Sometimes the precautions against drugging fail, and the horses which have been doped roll over in the path of others, causing spectacular pile-ups. On the sharp corners, even the most agile of horses break their legs (they are promptly shot).

In this air of feverish excitement, condemned by many outsiders as barbaric and cruel, bonds within the groups are reinforced by the sharing of intense, emotional experiences. The winning *contrada* celebrates with the ritual chanting of *"Daccelo!"* ("Give it to us!") as they struggle to touch the magical silk ribbon which is their prize and their collective glory. The losers steal away to spread rumours of unfair tactics and to comfort each other. Even in defeat, the members of a *contrada* are united by their sense of collective disappointment.

TROBRIAND CRICKET

In many ways the central sport spectacles in modern societies are clear reminders of our earlier cultural heritage. But, while we seem to have developed games from patterns of behaviour which are still evident in traditional societies, some tribal cultures have incorporated Western sports into their own ritual ceremonies and spectacles. A classic case is Trobriand cricket.

The Trobriand Islanders of New Guinea were originally investigated in the 1920s by one of the founding fathers of modern anthropology, Bronislaw Malinowski. His great concern at the time was that the influence of the West would eventually erode their traditional styles of behaviour and customs. The people themselves have, however, shown considerable resistance to the forces of acculturation. While they have not ignored Western influences, they have tended to adapt them so that they fit quite happily into the Trobrianders' traditional way of life.

Cricket was originally introduced to the islands by one of the early colonial administrators, who perhaps had in mind the peculiarly English idea that the game is "character-building". The Trobriand adaptation, however, is quite unlike the slow game – with its set of complex rules and special terms – from which it derived. It has become, instead, a noisy and large-scale celebration of good yam harvests which at the same time highlights rivalries between neighbouring villages.

There are no limits on how many men may play in each team, but there are attempts to make the numbers on each side roughly equal. The match is preceded by traditional war dances, but even these have modern, Western elements cleverly incorporated into them. One team, for example, might mimic an aircraft landing on the pitch, depositing soldiers with hand grenades and, with a clear touch of irony, a tourist. During the game, a batsman who is out is proclaimed "dead", and the opposing team chant "PK", referring to the sticky chewing gum. Although the score is kept using a tally of leaves, the result, in true Trobriand fashion, is that the home team always wins.

The Trobrianders are a living example of how change can come about at the same time that the essential ingredients of a tribal way of life are retained. Western goods are used in a manner which is appropriate to the traditional ways of doing things. While the white men – known as *dimdims* – exert an increasing influence on the economy, much of village life continues in a way which dates back to the Stone Age. Tractors may be in evidence, but pigs are still slaughtered using a stick hardened in a fire and driven through the heart. More importantly, each member of the community has a place, an identity and an active role to play in Trobriand society. In their version of cricket we see an example of how a society might enjoy the best of both worlds.

6 AGGRESSION AND WAR

An inevitable consequence of tribal bonding is hostility towards other tribes. A tribe gains its characteristic distinctiveness through contrasts with other groups, and having an "enemy" is one of the easiest ways of reinforcing the social ties which bind a community of people together. As we have developed from our hunter-gatherer roots, cooperation and aggression have grown together, a synergistic process which has both ensured our survival and created opportunities for group culture and individual social identity.

Mutual cooperation, and the processes of social bonding which go with it, arose from the need to hunt in the most effective way. In this sense cooperation was a pure adaptive feature of human behaviour and had a clear practical function. The social impact of such developments, however, was equally important. The emerging sense of solidarity and loyalty created tensions between neighbouring groups for two basic reasons. First, when food was scarce, there arose the need to protect the hunting grounds from the predatory activities of outsiders; territoriality was born. Second, in order to maintain tribal solidarity, tensions and frustrations needed to be channelled towards "out-groups" in order to reduce the risk of conflicts within the group. Rivalries with other tribes, for real or imagined reasons, created the kind of collective feeling which during World War II the British referred to as the "Dunkirk spirit". Through the depiction of outsiders as, as it were, Nazis, social unrest was reduced and tribal authority was rendered less vulnerable to challenge.

The process of claiming that foreign groups are unremittingly evil enemies is very evident today in our modern "super-tribes". Communism is the recurring *bête noire* of people in the United States. Iranians and Iraqis create mutually demonic images of each other as they compete for the resources of the Persian Gulf. Hostilities can be expressed in ways that seem to involve no aggression: the English tell jokes about the Irish, the French make fun of the Belgians, and the Poles in New York still bear the brunt of derisive humour. (Interestingly, the apparent butt of such jokes frequently turns the tables: the best Jewish jokes are told by Jews, and so forth.)

In many cases, modern conflicts are related to economic issues: to the need for cheap oil, better fishing grounds or primary industrial resources. But there are also strong social and cultural elements in the recurring conflicts between groups within the national units. While conflicts at the international scale threaten the very survival of the human race, the equivalent of tribal warfare in our modern societies has a quite separate function, and a very different prognosis.

TRADITIONAL WARFARE

As patterns of tribal warfare emerged to meet both practical and social requirements, there was an overriding need to develop means of limiting the potential destructiveness of this aggressive activity. If all skirmishes between

Opposite
Kenyan Masai stage a mock battle in which palm branches are used instead of spears.

Pages 132–3
Dani children learning the skills of hunting by playing spear-the-hoop, where the object is to aim a toy spear through a rolling and bouncing vine hoop.

rival tribes resulted in serious levels of fatalities, the risk of mutual annihilation would outweigh any potential benefits. If tribes needed enemies with which to contrast themselves favourably, then there was little to be gained from wiping out their rivals completely. For this, and for basic adaptive reasons, early warfare developed into a largely symbolic activity in which the point of the exercise was rarely to kill people, more to achieve dominance and control over them. In the way that conflicts within the group could be settled by ritual displays, songs, chants and dances, wars with other tribes came to be organized according to prescribed rules, ceremonies and mutually accepted codes of conduct.

A study made as recently as 1963 of the Dani of the New Guinea plains provides us with a classic example of the structure and function of tribal warfare. Although tribes such as the Dani are now rapidly being absorbed as a result of the forces of acculturation, their traditional modes of conflict and fighting serve as pointers to the roots of human aggression and provide us with insights into patterns of conflict that emerge unlikely corners of modern societies.

Traditional Dani culture is much concerned with the history of battles with the rival tribes which make up the plains population. Their history as warriors, however, was not built on the annexation of territory or the killing of enemies: war was never seen as having that purpose. The reasons for fighting were not, ostensibly, to do with practical or economic issues. The Dani fought because the ghosts of their dead ancestors bade them do so. All life in the New Guinea villages revolved around the influence of the ghosts. If things went wrong, crops failed or someone had an accident, then the ghosts were troubled. Going to war was seen as a way of calming the spirits and of preventing future calamities.

Such rationalizations for fighting may strike us as superstitious nonsense. But in fact the role of ghosts and spirits in traditional cultures is part of a folk heritage which makes perfect sense to members of the tribe. Needing to avenge the gods is as good a reason as any for a battle, so long as the warfare is conducted in a way which meets social requirements without causing extensive injury and death. The way in which the Dani fight their wars ensures that this is the case.

In a typical New Guinean plains skirmish, challenges are issued by small groups of warriors who are sent out in the early morning to the no-man's-lands which separate tribal territories. Such invitations to battle are invariably taken up, and preparations begin. The timing of the battle is discussed, with such important considerations as the weather forecast being taken into account. Indeed, the weather plays a big part in Dani warfare. Rain, in particular, is sufficient cause to abandon the fighting altogether. This is because the Dani prepare themselves for war using elaborate face-paint and decorations made from bird feathers: such decorations can be ruined by a sudden downpour and, since being dressed up in tribal regalia and adornment is vital to the entire ritual of warfare, battles can take place only on fine days.

The actual fighting, when it does occur, resembles an elaborate, ritual dance; it is an aggressive display rather than a seriously violent encounter. Sustained contact between the rival groups rarely lasts for more than ten minutes. Armed with spears or bows and arrows, warriors dart back and forth, but the risks to life and limb are quite limited. The death of a single tribesman is greeted as a major disaster and can bring the battle to a swift conclusion; even a serious injury is seen as being an extraordinary event. Anthropologists have found that the death toll from a year of war and fighting is usually 10–20 warriors, and this in a culture where battles are an everyday feature of normal existence.

The ultimate ritualization of warfare: the
Sealed Knot re-enact battles from the English
Civil War.

Above and opposite
Groups of young male warriors and their female followers dancing and chanting at a sing-sing festival in the Eastern Highlands of New Guinea.

This kind of tribal warfare is quite unlike its modern-day counterpart. The Dani have evolved a style of violence which explicitly limits the levels of death and injury. This is clear from the type of weapons used in fighting. Dani culture is steeped in a knowledge of birds and flight. Feathers and their properties are things that every member of the Dani tribe understands, yet the design of the arrows which they use in battles makes no use of this knowledge. The arrows have no flights and, as a result, it is very difficult to hit anything with them at a distance of more than 10 m. Since the failure to make the arrows fly more accurately cannot be attributed to a lack of knowledge, we have to assume that they are deliberately made so that they will not fly in a straight line. Attaching flights would make killing people a simple matter, but that is not the point of the exercise in Dani warfare. Instead, demonstrations of manly virtue and tribal solidarity can be conducted with less risk to the warriors than, say, death from the common cold.

MODERN RITUAL VIOLENCE

This process of limiting the conduct of violence within a social framework of rules and rituals has many parallels in the animal world. Many species of predatory animals have evolved very efficient means of killing their prey, ranging from sharp teeth and claws to antlers, horns and beaks. However, when the males fight other males of their own species in contests for dominance, basic resources or access to receptive females, such potentially lethal weaponry is rarely employed. Instead, ritualized fighting behaviours are displayed, in which a rival can be subdued without serious injury. Tribal cultures have developed the social equivalent of this process, and it is this pattern of aggressive behaviour which has likewise emerged in male youth cultures all over the modern world.

In Britain, various youth cultures have emerged since World War II, and most have been renowned for their aggressive behaviour. The Teddy Boys of the 1950s, the Mods and Rockers of the 1960s and the Skinheads of the early 1970s all gained reputations for anarchic violence and destruction. From the mid-1960s, soccer fans became the prime targets for media vilification as they

Group aggression is both generated and channelled by the style of music and the messages of the songs at this rock concert in London. The band is the Angelic Upstarts.

While British football fans have achieved an unenviable reputation for violence at football games, both at home and abroad, their contemporaries in other countries are by no means paragons of virtue. Here a French fan displays his violent potential.

established an image of senseless and gratuitous thuggery and destructiveness. The popular media, however, are rarely good guides to reality in such contexts, and detailed research has revealed quite a different aspect to youth-culture aggression.

Groups of football fans possessing almost obsessional allegiance to the teams which they fervently support not only have a clear social structure but also act within a strong framework of rules, conventions and rituals – those familiar hallmarks of tribal identification. What is most remarkable about their violent activities is the fact that the pattern is very close to that observed in traditional cultures. Outsiders are intimidated by their threatening postures, abusive language and violent threats, but in reality the number of serious injuries is remarkably low.

Research conducted in Britain has consistently shown that, although there are indeed many acts of violence committed by football fans in and around the stadia, the frequency and severity of these acts is not significantly above that which would be expected given a similar population of people in any other social context. A study in Scotland, for example, examined levels of reported crime, disturbance and vandalism in the areas where the football grounds are situated. A comparison was made between those Saturdays when football was played and those when it was not. The conclusion was that the football matches had no significant effect on levels of crime and violence. In some cases there were even indications that the football matches led to a reduction in these levels. It should be stressed that this research was conducted not by radical sociologists but by the police.

Some sporting events provide arenas for
social class rivalry. In England the "snobs"
at Derby Day are hassled by the "lads".

There are, of course, exceptions to the normal pattern of events. The 1985 tragedy in the Heysel stadium in Brussels, when 36 people, mainly fans of the Italian Juventus club, were killed after confrontations with Liverpool fans, still reminds us how things can go terribly wrong. Even here, however, the deaths were caused by panic reactions and a collapsing wall, not by the deliberately murderous acts of violent fans. While nobody can justifiably defend the violence which led up to that tragic loss of life, we must not fall into the trap of thinking that murder is a normal feature of football matches in Britain or anywhere else in Europe.

Aggression within groups of football fans is aroused in the stadia by the presence of fans of the rival team. These tend now to be segregated in a special area so that direct, physical clashes between the two factions are very difficult to achieve. The collective aggression serves to reinforce tribal solidarity, reaffirming social bonds and commitments among members of the soccer-terrace subculture. That aggression is, however, largely channelled into symbolic substitutes for violence. In the way that the Dani wage largely bloodless wars, the fans can enter into confrontations with their rivals every week without significant risk of serious injury to themselves or their peers, despite the image of bloodshed which surrounds their activity.

One major component of the soccer tribe's aggressive ritual is the use of stylized chants, which aim to denigrate their rivals. The interesting thing about these chants is that, while they are very insulting, they do not challenge the essential human quality of the opposition. Along with the chanting go stylized gestures, postures and facial expressions which provide further channels for the expression of hostility. The style of these expressions and the form of the gestures may seem trivial, but they are important clues to the type of aggression and violence which is to be expected.

However negatively we may view all kinds of fighting behaviour, the violence which occurs in these subcultures is essentially *social*, and is thus constrained by the tacit rules which accompany all social activities.

FIGHTING TO THE DEATH

This kind of ritual violence is not, of course, a panacea. There is always the risk of serious injury or death. Because of its ritual nature, it provides for the possibility of restraint, yet even in traditional societies tribal aggression can have serious consequences.

Among the Yanomamo of the Venezuela rain forests, for example, one out of four members of the male population dies as a result of combat. Known as the "Fierce People", the Yanomamo have the unenviable reputation of being the most violent in the world. Although many men are killed in battles and duels, there is still a shortage of females in the Yanomamo tribe, and so women are the cause of deadly feuds and rape is common. Wives are treated as negotiable commodities, and are generally subjected to repression and jealous guarding. The reason for the imbalance in the sexes is due to a rather perverse practice of selective infanticide. Male babies are held in great esteem, while daughters are considered to be reproductive failures and thus are often killed at birth. This in turn leads to the shortage of potential wives, a situation which gives rise to so much aggression among the males who compete for them.

This quirk of Yanomamo culture appears at first to be utterly irrational: after all, if the infanticide practice were to be abandoned, then the root cause of much of the males' violence would disappear with it. However, there is perhaps a strange logic in the system. Although the Yanomamo are surrounded by abundant vegetation, there is a shortage of animal protein in the ecology. As a result, there are frequent skirmishes with neighbouring tribes over the matter of hunting territories. In order to hold his own in this competitive world, there is a need for the Yanomamo male to be a skilled fighter with an appropriate level of fierceness and determination. Through the production of a state of affairs whereby there are too few females, these warlike tendencies in the males can be guaranteed.

The high levels of violence among the Yanomamo can be seen as a practical solution to problems which arise when there is a shortage of basic resources. The Dani, with their abundance of crops and rich hunting territories, have no need to kill members of rival tribes and have therefore adapted their style of warfare to prevent bloodshed. Tribal aggression remains, serving to reinforce social bonds, but lacks the counterproductive deadliness.

In modern tribes we see the same contrasts. Where there is no fundamental *need* for injurious violence, fighting is ritualized, becoming little more than a symbolic display. In harsher economic climates, however, the pattern of violence can change, and there are signs that this may be occurring in the soccer culture. With increased youth unemployment and social alienation, the ritual framework is often unable to contain the aggression. Violence of a quite different and essentially non-social kind is therefore emerging. This is true also in the case of street gangs in the major cities of the United States.

US youth gangs are highly distinctive tribal groups, occupying strictly delimited territories in major urban areas. In New York, for example, there are about 400 different gangs, the total membership of which is estimated to be anywhere between 10,000 and 40,000. A typical gang in Brooklyn or the Bronx might occupy a territory only a few blocks square, taking care to avoid neighbouring streets staked out by a rival tribe. Members of the more established gangs signify their membership by wearing the gang's distinctive "colours" – elaborately designed emblems and logos attached to their clothing.

The ostensible function of these gangs is to defend their neighbourhood from the criminal activities of outsiders. Gang members talk at length about the valuable social roles they play in the community and about the brotherhood which exists between them. They talk of protecting the community and of helping the poor and the oppressed. The reality, however, is rather different from the "Robin Hood" image which they seek to project. Many gang members control local narcotic sales and distribution, and protection rackets, involving the extortion of local shopkeepers, are common.

Inter-gang violence is a relatively uncommon event, but when it occurs it can result in serious injuries and even fatalities. Virtually all gang members carry weapons such as shotguns, machetes, switch-blade knives and baseball bats, and the tribal rules for fighting are quite different from those found among British football fans. There are, however, similarities in the basic values associated with aggressive conflicts. Gang members speak of "heart" – the courage to stand up for oneself and one's group and to defend the reputation and image of the gang. In many ways the concepts of manly pride, bravery and unflinching commitment in the face of personal danger parallel those found in European youth cultures and in most traditional cultures. However, whereas the rules and rituals of the soccer subculture constrain violence within largely non-injurious displays, the rules within the gangs appear to have the opposite effect.

In most British youth groups, the use of a weapon is generally seen as a form of cowardice, especially if one's rival is unarmed. Their US counterparts, however, subscribe to a different philosophy. To challenge a member of a rival gang without taking the precaution of carrying a weapon is considered to be "dumb". Similarly, in group conflicts, gangs will often try to predict what kind of weapons their rivals will be using so that they can go prepared with something yet more deadly. As one New York gang member put it: "You're going to go down there and rumble and they got baseball bats – what you gonna do? You gonna go with bats? No, you're gonna take lead [shotguns]."

The rules of gang violence are designed to ensure survival but at the same time they are rooted in practical considerations. Just as the Yanomamo compete with their neighbours for access to vital resources, the street gangs struggle to maintain the level and success of their criminal activities in the territories which they control. Both types of tribal group share common values and patterns of ritual behaviour; however, when times are hard and there is more than just honour at stake, killing becomes a legitimized mode of behaviour.

SCAPEGOATS

European youth tribes, while perpetuating a style of aggressive expression which has much in common with the relatively "safe" warfare of the Dani and other traditional cultures, have recently begun in some cases to escalate their levels of injurious violence. We have seen this occurring on the soccer terraces of Britain and among the Stifosi and Ultras of Italian football stadia. Italian fans, having

Tribalism in its ugly modern guise. A group of young French fascist Skinheads in the streets of Paris.

borrowed much of their style from their British counterparts, have created clans and tribes which are very similar in many ways to their street-gang contemporaries in New York and Los Angeles. While it is the British fans who are portrayed in the world's media as the "disease" of international soccer, Italian fans can pose a greater threat to life and limb on their home territories.

Many of the Italian soccer tribes have adopted neo-Nazi styles, and their mode of fighting often reflects their extreme political views. Theirs is the violence of alienated youth looking for easy scapegoats. It flows not from the process of tribal bonding but from the lack of identity and personal involvement characteristic of our over-large modern societies. The return to tribalism is here a defensive reaction – one which fosters, rather than constrains, the anger and frustrations of daily life.

At a typical football game in Naples today the stadium is surrounded by armed police, some toting machine-guns; water cannon and armoured vans and lorries equipped with teargas-grenade launchers are on hand. Inside the ground, further armed police and soldiers pack sections of the terracing, and even the stewards in the press room carry revolvers. Fans are separated from the playing field by a dry moat 12 m (40 ft) deep. Players have access to the field only through a heavily guarded tunnel which emerges by the touch line. Such precautions, claim the football authorities, are essential in order to prevent not just fights between rival factions but deadly attacks on players and officials. Because of all this fortification, the Italian football clans have little opportunity for physical contact with their rivals, and so must vent their aggression through symbolic displays. These can be frightening in their intensity. Unlike their British counterparts, who rely principally on songs, chants and gestures, the Ultras pound tribal drums constantly throughout the game, set fire to rubbish on the terraces, and create an almost impenetrable fog using smoke flares and fireworks.

The fascist overtones of many Italian youth groups, which strongly influence the pattern of tribal violence, are to be found also in some French subcultures. Skinheads in Paris, like football fans in Italy, have taken their inspiration from British youth culture, but inflict higher levels of injury on their victims. The so-called Nazi Klan is one of the most notorious of Parisian youth tribes; it took its style from the British Punk movement of the late 1970s. On the football terraces the tribe members are clearly identifiable by their shouts of "Sieg Heil" and their Nazi-style salutes. In the streets of the Saint Michel quarter their routine activities revolve around beating up immigrants and acts of apparently quite gratuitous savagery. They control the catacombs and empty Metro corridors, and treat anyone found there as a violator of their tribal territory.

The violence of the Nazi Klan is that of the urban guerrilla – a tribal response to perceived oppression and victimization. In this kind of warfare there are few constraints, and encounters with rivals are essentially nonsocial in nature. Just as the British Skinheads directed their hostilities toward identifiable outgroups, such as homosexuals and the Asian community, the neo-fascist youth groups in Europe tend to prey on those whom they have identified as responsible for their own depressed situation. By creating an "enemy" whom they can blame, they develop group bonds which insulate them from the reality of their plight.

This process of creating tribal solidarity through the victimization of others has been very evident in the history and development of the Ku Klux Klan, the racist organization for long prevalent in the southern United States. Born in the aftermath of the Civil War, the KKK adopted ritual dress and codes of conduct specifically in order to instil terror into the Black population. By depicting Blacks as racially inferior, the members of the KKK – drawn almost exclusively from the poor white classes, or "white trash", as the Blacks dubbed them – were able to perceive of themselves as an elevated caste, even though their economic, educational and other circumstances were dire in comparison with those enjoyed elsewhere in the United States.

After World War I, when the KKK experienced a revival in terms of membership, other categories of "alien" scapegoats were added to their list of outsiders. W. J. Simmons, who led the reconstructed Klan, used his skills as a preacher to whip up tribal hostility towards not only Blacks but also Roman Catholics, Jews and people with left-wing political views. Violence, lynchings and carefully directed thuggery hid behind a veneer of respectable Protestant conservatism as much as they did behind the rather ludicrous white hoods and masks.

The same process – establishment of group solidarity through the vilification and persecution of others – is evident in the British Skinhead tribes and related youth subcultures. Like the KKK in the United States, and their new converts in Britain, members of the white working classes are alienated from a society in which they have failed to achieve status. Their frustration is vented on

An awesome sense of intimidation is created by the fascist salutes at an Italian football match.

identifiable groups which they believe, for no logical reason, to be instrumental in their lack of achievement. Asian immigrants are cast in the same role as that of the Jews in Nazi Germany. Tribal lore of the Skinhead culture assigns blame to such outsiders, and thereby legitimizes violence against them.

LIMITS OF TRIBAL VIOLENCE

There are two modes of aggression to which tribal loyalties can lead: quite harmless rituals, on the one hand, and violence of a savage and ruthless nature, on the other. The primary factor dictating the manner in which tribal hostilities are expressed is essentially economic. When groups lack a sense of hope for a better future and material welfare, their collective violence approaches that of the Yanomamo. When basic needs are met, and individuals within the groups are able to establish a true sense of worth and respect, the aggression engendered by inter-tribe conflicts takes on the innocuous style of Dani warfare. The Yanomamo are forced to raid, pillage and kill because of the lack of freely available protein. The relatively well-off Dani can afford to "play at being warriors" because all that is at stake is pride.

As we have seen, there are limitations to the extent to which tribal violence is allowed to escalate. Tribal bonds may be responsible for the creation of particular hostile attitudes and the direction of aggression toward specific targets. But those same bonds also provide the means for constraining violence. Tribal violence is essentially *social* violence, involving direct interaction and understanding between the protagonists. Violence in the form of massacre and genocide occurs primarily because those social forces have been eroded to the point where they are no longer effective as constraints. This has happened during periods of colonization of traditional cultures by Western powers. In the face of an enemy intent on the destruction of a viable way of tribal life, the defence has been bloody in the extreme.

Modern warfare, as waged between nations, is an example of impersonal, non-tribal violence, and its consequences are inevitably far more bloody than the battles waged by traditional societies. Could this, however, be simply due to the levels of technology involved? With modern weaponry, an individual in the United States could destroy an entire city in the Soviet Union with just one press of a button. There is little potential for direct social involvement, and the constraints which accompany it, in such a lethal action.

While the technology of modern warfare can account for both its deadliness and its impersonal nature, there is more to the story. The fact that we can even contemplate using such tools of destruction suggests that our social organization has become far removed from its tribal heritage. As we noted (see page 134), the Dani of New Guinea, for all their understanding of feathers and flight, do not put this knowledge to use in the design of their weapons of war. The North American Plains Indians provide us with an even clearer example of tribal approaches to arms limitation. Their culture was steeped in the traditions of hunting. To survive and prosper, weapons were developed which were very efficient at killing buffalo and other animals. These weapons, of course, represented a significant advance on previous methods of killing large animals, such as driving them over the edge of a cliff. With the bow-and-arrow, prey could be stalked and shot on the spot as and when required. Equally, however, this new-found technology could be put to use in the killing of other people and in the waging of war with rival tribes. Yet the bow-and-arrow was never developed as a man-killing tool, even though the knowledge and potential for such an adaptation were certainly there. Buffalo have ribs which run vertically. In order to kill them it was logical to mount the flint arrowheads so that they were in line with the bow-string notch on the other end of the arrow – i.e., vertically. Used in this way, the arrows could easily pass through the buffalo's ribcage and bring about its swift demise.

Humans have, of course, horizontal ribs. To use the bow-and-arrow as a weapon of war would therefore have required only a simple modification of the orientation of the arrowheads. When metal tips (largely cut from the discarded frying pans of white settlers) became available, there was the opportunity to make this weaponry even more deadly in the conduct of war. Yet the essential adaptations were never made. The bow-and-arrow was for hunting and killing prey. Warfare was more a matter of seeking honour and reputation than of the simple slaying of rival warriors.

In tribal societies the ways in which honour and reputation are gained in battles and confrontation are strictly determined by cultural traditions and rules. In most of the North American Indian tribes, the prescribed method was that of "counting coup". The aim was to ride up to an enemy and hit him on the head with one's bare hand, or perhaps with the bow; some tribes had special coup sticks for this ritual purpose, but the principle was just the same. Honour was quite unrelated to the severity of the injury inflicted, instead being bestowed on those who showed courage and fearlessness coupled with an act of violence so limited in its impact that it was almost purely symbolic.

Such rituals of violence were only possible, of course, because the warrior knew that his enemy was also more intent on counting coup than on attempting to kill him. Warfare depended on a mutual trust between the two sets of protagonists. Exactly the same is true in modern tribal conflicts. The aggressive rituals of British football fans revolve around the use of stylized gestures and chants. As we have seen, the interesting thing about these chants is that, while insulting, they do not challenge the essential human quality of the opposition. Rarely, for example, are opposing fans described as animals, and nor are animalist qualities usually ascribed to them. For honour to be achieved, a rival has to be afforded similar status to oneself. To understand how large-scale violence in modern societies can become such a destructive and impersonal disaster, we need to understand how our hunting ancestry can rear its head in a quite unexpected manner.

THE HUNTING FACTOR

The importance of our hunting ancestry is difficult to overstate. The anthropologist Robin Fox sees this aspect of our biological and cultural evolution as pervading all aspects of modern living. He points out that the model of "civilized" Man, based on our recent history in industrialized societies, is too shallow for a true understanding of our patterns of behaviour. To discover our true nature, we

Hunting whales is still very much part of the way of life among the people of Baffin Island.

Above
Grouse shooting in Britain is an expensive activity for the upper classes. Most of the grouse are specially bred and nurtured to provide sport for those who can afford the fees charged by the landowners.

Left
Crocodile hunting as still practised by the Palau of Micronesia.

Right
Fox hunting in England is one of the most ritualized of all hunting activities, involving initiation ceremonies in which novices have the blood of a newly killed fox rubbed on their faces. In the more traditional hunts, full members wear the traditional red jackets, which are known as "pinks".

Below
Stalking wild pigs, as practised by the Urueu-Wau-Wau Indians in South America.

have to look much further back in our developmental sequence:

> We remain Upper Paleolithic hunters, fine-honed machines designed for the efficient pursuit of game. Nothing worth noting has happened in our evolutionary history since we left off hunting and took to the fields and towns – nothing except perhaps a little selection for immunity to epidemics, and probably not even that. "Man the hunter" is not an episode from our distant past: we are still the hunter, incarcerated, domesticated, polluted, crowded and bemused.

Fox and others argue that our evolution as hunters is still evident in our basic genetic and biological make-up. Our brains remain wired-up to hunt, even though our habitats and circumstances have been radically altered. The evidence for this is, to say the least, rather speculative. But whether because of biological or basic cultural forces, the notion that we remain hunters in the modern world helps us to understand core features of our social and political behaviour.

While the hunting of animals remains as a functional activity in many traditional societies, essential for physical survival, it takes on quite different forms in modern societies. Our predatory tendencies are clearly evident in the world of small business, where entrepreneurs employ the same psychological processes and skills as their distant ancestors on the African plains. We have seen how modern sports have developed to provide an outlet for seemingly redundant

physical attributes and skills. But perhaps the most direct reflection of this central aspect of tribal heritage lies in our continuing desire to hunt and kill animals even when such activities rarely provide any functional advantage.

Recreational hunting is essentially a male, group activity. It brings together individuals with a common purpose in a cooperative activity. Occasionally the activity is given an ostensible rationale, such as the need to control the fox population or to cull male deer. Such explanations, however, are usually unconvincing and fail to mask the true purpose of the exercise – the display of manly skills in a closely-bonded social context. It is also the case that it is in the most wealthy countries that hunting and game fishing are most commonly practised. The anthropologist Lionel Tiger notes that the desire of men in affluent societies to re-create the food-gathering conditions of people in traditional cultures bears witness to the strength of the hunting drives.

The persistence of hunting drives in modern societies can, however, present problems. Because of the scale and impersonality of many modern societies, predatory violence can be directed not only against animals but also, in some circumstances, against other people.

In order that tribal aggression and violence can be conducted within a constraining social framework, it is essential that they are clearly distinguished from hunting activities, where the animal targets can be killed without ceremony. The Omaha Indians had a word for war, *nuatathishon*, which highlighted this separation and dictated the kinds of activity in which warriors

Above
The ceremonial trophies of past hunts, displayed here by the Duc and Duchesse de Brissac in their country home.

Top
Stag hunting in France involves not only chases across fields and woodland but also in the rivers.

Fishing, as practised by the Colombian Turkana, who use bows and spears.

could legitimately engage. *Nuatathishon* meant "war with men"; more particularly, it referred to fights with other adult males. Children and women were specifically excluded from the category of persons against whom violence could be directed. The nature of the violence itself was likewise strictly codified, enforcing relatively non-injurious behaviours and a constant regard for the essential humanity of the enemy.

The lack of dehumanization so characteristic of tribal warfare is found also in many youth tribes of the modern cultures. Rather than referring to rivals and enemies as "animals", and therefore to be hunted, they instead operate a process of demasculinization. The male enemy is still a fellow human, but his masculinity is symbolically taken away from him. Thus the chants of the soccer tribes commonly suggest that rivals are homosexual, have small genitalia and masturbate frequently. The "home" tribe is, by contrast, described in the singing

and chanting as actively heterosexual, with considerable manly virtues and sexual appetite. Exactly similar links between sexuality and aggression are to be found in traditional societies. The Dani warrior, for example, exaggerates the size of his genitalia by wearing an enormous penis-sheath in battle: some of these are well over a metre long!

The greatest irony is, perhaps, that the legacy of our hunting past should surface primarily in modern societies which have grown too vast for tribal bonds to be maintained in mainstream structures. While traditional societies rule out the possibility of predatory behaviour in conflicts with their fellow human beings, modern warfare is characterized not only by its technological sophistication but also by the awesome lethality which arises when we can regard people as subhuman and therefore legitimate objects for our predatory drives.

To realize the full horror which results from our shift away from the social nature of tribal violence, we have only to examine events in the recent history of Western societies. One stands out like an unhealed scar on the collective human consciousness: the systematic extermination of up to six million Jews and an untold number of gypsies, homosexuals, "asocials" and others in the concentration camps of Nazi Germany. It is sometimes assumed that the German guards responsible for the operation of the gas chambers of Auschwitz and Belsen were brutish savages driven by a lust for death and destruction. In reality, however, many were perfectly ordinary people caught up in a collective pattern of activity which can only come about in a non-tribal context. The whole business of mass

The burning cross and the robes of the Ku Klux Klan, seen here at a National Convention in Connecticut in 1986, are tribal emblems designed to instil fear in the targets of this sinister organization's hatred.

The alienation and despair experienced in the slums of Mexico City suburbs are vented in street violence by these groups of Punks.

extermination was carried out in a methodical and detached manner. The Jews were not subjected to the crazed attacks of foaming savages. They were marshalled into chambers disguised as shower rooms and, without excitement, poisoned or suffocated.

Such horrendous acts can be conducted with so little concern only when the targets have been successfully reduced to a subhuman status. If the naked, frail and trembling figure before you is no longer a person but an animal, his or her death is of as little consequence as that of the poisoned rat or the vermin which can be crushed to extinction with ease, and even with enthusiasm. For example, we can subject an entire rabbit population to the slow, grisly death of myxomatosis with few protests being heard: we argue that the rabbits eat the food in the fields, destroy crops and cost the farmers money. Once people have, as it were, been converted into rabbits, their death is equally of little concern. The way in which they are killed becomes unimportant if they are perceived to be posing a threat to the progress of the super-tribe – or, in the case of the Nazis, to Aryan domination.

The hunting factor, coupled with our unique ability to symbolically transform the nature of the targets of our aggression, allows us to do things which would otherwise be unthinkable. Dehumanization, however, is not something which can be achieved overnight. Even within the faceless and anonymous contexts of our modern societies, our tribal heritage naturally forces us to consider even our fiercest enemies as essentially human. The transformation is achieved because of two key features of the national cultures in which we live.

The first of these is the impersonal pattern of authority so characteristic of our societies. One of the commonest defences at the Nuremberg trials was that those charged with committing acts of atrocity were simply following the orders of their superiors. The case of Lieutenant Calley, responsible for the My Lai massacre in Vietnam in 1968, likewise centred on whether or not he had been following a statutory obligation when he ordered the killing of hundreds of innocent Vietnamese families. This pattern of authority relations does not, in itself, lead to unmitigated violence. A soldier ordered to shoot his own comrade for no apparent reason might well refuse, whatever the cost to himself. Yet authority of this kind can control the process of symbolically transforming particular groups of people into animals or even objects – a process known as routinization.

The term "routinization" refers to the use of language and the ways in which people are described. We have only to examine the Nazi propaganda of the 1930s to see how easily a race of people can be held responsible for all of a society's ills, and therefore subsequently reduced to the status of a lesser breed. There were constant references to Jews as "vermin", "reptiles", "swine" and "filthy animals". There was also a lot made of the Jews' alleged animalistic behaviour. They were accused of eating their own children and of engaging in incest, two taboos from which a normal human being would shrink. When Field-Marshal von Reichenau issued statements to his juniors such as "a soldier must have an understanding of the necessity of a severe but just revenge on subhuman Jewry" he was contributing to the process which served ultimately to legitimize the enactment of the Final Solution. At the same time he was following very closely the guidelines laid down by the SS, the *Sprachregelungen*, or "language rules". These comprised a highly codified set of instructions as to how the business of extermination and destruction was to be described, and how the victims were to be labelled. The term "Final Solution" was part of this bureaucratic transform-ation of reality. It is not easy to live with words such as "mass extermination", "murder" and "torture", because they arouse immediate revulsion; terms such as "special treatment" and "evacuation", on the other hand, disguise the true reality of the violence being perpetrated. Through the careful use of language, we transform not only the status of the victims but also our perception of the acts we commit.

Such transformations, which can be achieved only in modern societies with large, impersonal bureaucracies, constitute the basic difference between tribal and modern war. The new technology of today's weaponry adds to the destructive power of warfare but is not, in itself, responsible for our capacity for mass killing. It is when we become hunters who lack a tribe that we achieve the dubious distinction of being the most murderous species alive.

BIBLIOGRAPHY

Angeloglou, M., *A History of Make-Up*, Studio-Vista, London, 1970

Atkinson, J. M., "The effectiveness of shamans in an Indonesian ritual", *American Anthropologist*, 89, 1987

Barr, A. and York, P., *The Official Sloane Ranger Handbook*, St Martin, London, 1983

Barrett, L. E., *The Rastafarians: The Dreadlocks of Jamaica*, Sangster's/Heinemann, Kingston

Bogdanor, V. and Skidelsky, R. (eds), *The Age of Affluence*, Macmillan, London, 1970

Boyd, D. J., "The commercialization of ritual in the Eastern Highlands of Papua New Guinea", *Man* (N.S.), 20, 325–40

Brake, M., *Comparative Youth Culture*, Routledge and Kegan Paul, London, 1985

Broby-Johansen, R., *Body and Clothes*, Faber, London, 1968

Calder, N., *The Human Conspiracy*, BBC, London, 1976

Cameron, A., *Circus Factions: Blues and Greens at Rome and Byzantium*, Oxford University Press, Oxford, 1976

Campbell, A., *The Girls in the Gang*, Blackwell, New York, 1984

Caudrey, A., "Greenham – the survival camp", *New Society*, 4 April 1986

Caudrey, A., "Respectable sisters", *New Society*, 18 October 1985

Chagnon, N., *Yanomamo – The Fierce People*, Holt, Rinehart and Winston, New York, 1977

Chambers, I., *Popular Culture: The Metropolitan Experience*, Methuen, London, 1986

Charsley, S., "What does a wedding cake mean?", *New Society*, 3 July 1987

Cheska, A. T., "Sports Spectacular: The Social Ritual of Power", in Hart and Birrell (eds), *op. cit.*

Cohen, S., *Folk Devils and Moral Panics*, MacGibbon and Kee, London, 1972

Eibl-Eibesfeldt, I., *The Biology of Peace and War*, Thames and Hudson, London, 1979

Elkin, A. P., *The Australian Aborigines*, Doubleday, New York, 1964

Fiske, S., "Pigskin Review: An American Institution" in Hart and Birrell (eds), *op. cit.*

Flugel, J. C., *The Psychology of Clothes*, Hogarth Press, London, 1930

Forty, A., *Objects of Desire*, Thames and Hudson, London, 1986

Fox, R., *Encounter with Anthropology*, Harcourt, Brace, Jovanovich, New York, 1973

Gardner, R. and Heider, K. G., *Gardens of War*, André Deutsch, London, 1969

Geertz, C., "Deep Play: Notes on the Balinese Cockfight", *Daedalus* 1–37, 1972

Gillis, J., "Weddings great and small", *New Society*, 18 July 1986

Gmelch, S. B., "Groups that don't want in: Gypsies and other artisan, trader, and entertainer minorities", *Annual Review of Anthropology*, 15, 307–330, 1986

Goody, J. R., *Production and Reproduction: A Comparative Study of the Domestic Domain*, Cambridge University Press, Cambridge, 1977

Hall, S. *et al.* (eds), *Resistance Through Rituals*, Hutchinson, London, 1976

Hammond, D., *Associations*, Addison-Wesley, Reading, Massachusetts, 1972

Harris, M., "The Doc Marten Angels", *New Society*, 24 May 1984

Hart, G., "The Droppies", *New Society*, 5 September 1986

Hart, M. and Birrell, S. (eds), *Sport in the Sociocultural Process*, William C. Brown, Dubuque, Iowa, 1981

Haviland, W. A., *Cultural Anthropology*, Holt, Rinehart and Winston, New York, 1983

Heald, S., "The making of men: the relevance of vernacular psychology to the interpretation of a Gisu Ritual", *Africa*, 52(1), 1982

Heald, S., "The Ritual Use of Violence: Circumcision among the Gisu of Uganda", in Riches (ed), *op. cit.*

Hebdige, D., *Subculture: The Meaning of Style*, Methuen, London, 1979

Hebdige, D., "Reggae, Rastas and Rudies", in S. Hall *et al.* (eds), *op. cit.*

Howard, M., *War in European History*, Oxford University Press, Oxford, 1976

Howard, M. C., *Contemporary Cultural Anthropology*, Little, Brown and Co., Boston, 1986

Jefferson, T., "The cultural meaning of the Teds", in S. Hall *et al.* (eds), *op. cit.*

Kaplan, D. E. and Dubro, A., *Yakuza*, Macdonald, London, 1987

Kelman, H., "Violence without moral restraint", *Journal of Social Issues*, 9, 1973

Knight, S., *The Brotherhood*, Grafton, London, 1985

Knipe, H. and Maclay, G., *The Dominant Man*, Souvenir Press, London, 1972

Kondo, D., "The way of tea: A symbolic analysis", *Man* (N.S.) 20, 287–306

La Fontaine, J. S. (ed), *The Interpretation of Ritual*, Tavistock, London, 1972

La Fontaine, J. S., *Initiation: Ritual Drama and Secret Knowledge Across the World*, Penguin, Harmondsworth, 1985

Leakey, R. E., *Origins*, Macdonald and Jane's, London, 1977

Little, K., "The role of voluntary associations in West African Urbanization", in Van den Berghe (ed), *op. cit.*

Lomax, D., "The Freemasons", *The Listener*, 21 May 1987

Lowenberg, M. E. *et al.*, *Food and People*, Wiley, New York, 1979.

Marsh, P., *Aggro: The Illusion of Violence*, Dent & Son, London, 1978

Marsh, P. and Collett, P., *Driving Passion: The Psychology of the Car*, Jonathan Cape, London 1986

Marsh, P., Harre, R. and Rosser, E., *Rules of Disorder*, Routledge and Kegan Paul, London, 1968

Marvin, G., "Honour, Integrity and the Problem of Violence in the Spanish Bullfight", in Riches (ed), *op. cit.*

Miller, W. B., *Violence by Youth Gangs and Youth Groups as a Crime Problem in Major American Cities*, U.S. Government Printing Office, Washington D.C., 1975

Moorehead, C., "The women of Japan", *New Society*, 20 December 1984

Morris, D., *The Naked Ape*, Jonathan Cape, London, 1967

Morris, D., *The Soccer Tribe*, Jonathan Cape, London, 1981

Morris, D., *Bodywatching*, Jonathan Cape, London, 1985

Morris, D., Collett, P., Marsh, P. and O'Shaughnessy, M., *Gestures: Their Origins and Distribution*, Jonathan Cape, London, 1979

Newman, O., *Defensible Space*, Macmillan, New York, 1973

Panton, L., "Polygamy – the 'honest way' of taking a partner", *The Listener*, 15 August 1985

Pliny (the Younger), *Letters*, Book IX, 6, Oxford University Press, Oxford, 1963

Polhemus, T. (ed), *Social Aspects of the Human Body*, Penguin, Harmondsworth, 1978

Riches, D. (ed), *The Anthropology of Violence*, Blackwell, Oxford, 1986

Rutherford, P., *The Druids – Magicians of the West*, Aquarian Press, Wellingborough, 1983

Sagan, C., "Game – The prehistoric origin of sport", *Parade*, 13 September 1987

Shapiro, H. (ed), *Man, Culture and Society*, Oxford University Press, New York, 1960

Sudjic, D., *Cult Objects*, Paladin, London, 1985

Sweeny, J., "Disarray among the masons", *New Society*, 28 March 1986

Thompson, H., *Hell's Angels*, Random House, New York, 1966

Tiger, L., *Men in Groups*, Thomas Nelson, London, 1969

Tiger, L. and Fox, R., *The Imperial Animal*, Secker and Warburg, London, 1972.

Topouzis, D., "The men with many wives", *New Society*, 4 October 1985.

Van den Berghe, P. (ed.), *Africa: Social Problems of Change and Conflict*, Chandler, San Francisco, 1964

Van Gennep, A., *The Rites of Passage*, The University of Chicago Press, Chicago, 1960

Willis, P., *Profane Culture*, Routledge and Kegan Paul, London, 1978

York, P., *Style Wars*, Sidgwick and Jackson, London, 1983

York, P., *Modern Times*, Heinemann, London, 1986

Young, F. W., *Initiation Ceremonies: A Cross-Cultural Study of Status Dramatization*, Bobbs-Merrill, Indianapolis, 1965

Zurcher, L. A. and Meadow, A., "On bullfights and baseball: An example of interaction of social institutions", *International Journal of Comparative Sociology*, 8, 99–117, 1967

Index

Page numbers in *italics* refer to relevant captions.

ACKNOWLEDGEMENTS

A special thank you to Francesca Kenny for her background research and kind assistance in many ways, and thanks also to Desmond Morris, the tribal elder, for his continuing flow of good ideas.

PICTURE CREDITS

All-Sport 44–5 (© C. Cole), 112, 114–15, 117, 123 (© M. Passmore), 140; Black Star 120–21 (© J. Launois); Colorific! 53, 55, 66 above, 67, 69, 80, 101, 131, 149 below, 151 above, 153; Sally and Richard Greenhill 76; Robert Harding Picture Library 12, 13 below, 15 (© Lomax), 38, 61, 63, 68 (© I. Griffiths), 71, 73, 75, 78 left and above, 85, 102, 136 (© I. Griffiths), 137 (© I. Griffiths); Harvard University 132–3; Hutchison Library 16, 23, 28 (© W. Jesko v. Puttkamer), 29, 36, 37, 43 (© M. MacIntyre), 50, 51, 56, 65 right, 70 (© M. MacIntyre), 79 left, 81, 87 below, 116, 148, 150 left, 152; Impact Photos 13 above (© M. Cator), 22 (© B. Harris), 57 above (© M. Cator), 65 below (© C. Pillitz), 66 below (© M. Cator), 74 (© J. Fraser), 86 (© M. Cator), 104 (© A. le Garsmeur), 110 (© H. Sykes), 119 (© J. Nicholl), 141 (© M. Cator), 149 above (© M. Cator), 150 above (© M. Cator); Independent Newspaper Publishing 11 above; Italian State Tourist Office, London 128; Magnum 59 (© J. Gaumy); Peter Marsh 11 below, 138–9; Pictorial Press 79 right; Rex Features Ltd, London 25 above and below, 106–7, 124, 125, 135, 151 right; Frank Spooner Pictures (© Gamma) 14 left and right, 19, 24, 35, 40, 52, 57 below, 60, 62 right and above, 82, 83, 105, 144, 154; Times Newspapers Ltd 146; Topham Picture Library 64, 87 above (© *The Observer*) 94–5; Transworld Feature Syndicate (UK) Ltd 20; Zefa Picture Library 17, 32 below, 41 (© D. Baglin), 54 (© B. Leidmann), 89 (© R. Bond), 90 (© A. J. Brown), 99 (© H. Siefnmans).